To Rochelle,

A sensitive lady. May
this help you to continue
to help others.

Myra F. Lenck
July 21, 1991

Mommy, Daddy, Look What I'm Saying

Mommy, Daddy, Look What I'm Saying:

What Children Are Telling You through Their Art

DR. MYRA F. LEVICK

WITH DIANA S. WHEELER

M. Evans and Company, Inc.   New York

The author and publisher thank Charles C. Thomas, Publisher, and Gardner Press, Inc., for the release of some drawings used in this book.

Library of Congress Cataloging-in-Publication Data
Levick, Myra F.
  Mommy, daddy, look what I'm saying.

  Bibliography: p.
  Includes index.
  1. Drawing, Psychology of.   2. Child psychology.
  3. Child psychopathology.   4. Child development.
  I. Wheeler, Diana S.   II. Title.
  BF723.D7L465   1986   155.4   85-25916

  ISBN 0-87131-462-2

M. Evans and Company, Inc.
216 East 49 Street
New York, New York 10017

Design by James L. McGuire

Manufactured in the United States of America
9 8 7 6 5 4 3 2 1

To my mother, Ida,
and
my daughters,
Bonnie, Karen, and Marsha

Contents

Acknowledgments

The idea of writing this book was not mine; those who will benefit from it should credit my husband, Leonard. While I hesitated to initiate this venture, he argued that many art therapists, including myself, have over the years frequently spoken to parents' and teachers' groups, explaining in simple language what art therapy is. He suggested that I transform *They Could Not Talk and So They Drew,* the textbook for professionals that I had written and published in 1983, into a book that could be used by those who are primarily involved in caring for children. I accepted my husband's challenge and completed this work, but that could not have been accomplished without his continual encouragement, patience, and love.

I thank Israel Zwerling, M.D., Ph.D., and Interim Dean of the School of Medicine at Hahnemann University, who also encouraged me to pursue this and suggested that I include a discussion of normal children's behavior for each stage of development. This elaboration enhanced the original concept.

My brother, Rick Friedman, a former newspaper editor and now free-lance writer, was most helpful in developing the first draft of the proposal for this work.

I thank Alice Fried Martell for her patience and guidance in the preparation of the final draft of the proposal and the outline, for her continued encouragement throughout the writing of this book, and for her leading me to M. Evans and Company, Inc., which is the publisher of this book.

I was most fortunate to have Diana Wheeler edit as I wrote, in order to help me maintain the presentation I was striving for. I was even more fortunate in that, as we progressed, she became as enthusiastic as I was about this material. We learned a great deal from each other in the process.

This work could not have been completed on time without the help of Georgina Wells. Georgina is not only a superb typist and a "whiz" at word processing, but she is also a very bright and sensitive young woman. Her interest and responsiveness to our goals provided us with an astute "third pair of eyes" in the final proofreading of this manuscript.

Without the children and without the parents and teachers who shared stories and pictures about and by their children, this book could not have been written. To preserve confidentiality, I cannot mention their names, but they know who they are, and I thank them for their contributions, interest, and support of this work.

I particularly appreciate the consideration and understanding I have received from Linda Cabasin and Herb Katz at M. Evans and Company, in the preparation of this work in a way that I believe meets the needs of parents and teachers.

Finally, I thank my mother, children, and grandchildren for their constant support and encouragement of my endeavors. They make it possible for me to work and to love.

Introduction

WHAT YOU CAN LEARN FROM THIS BOOK

Figure 1

This drawing (figure 1) of a floating house was created by a 5½-year-old-boy. To the untrained eye, it would appear to be a typical child's drawing. The house has a door, windows, and a roof. To the eye of the art therapist, however, there are several things wrong. There is no smoke coming out of the chimney—in fact, there is no chimney at all. There are no people in the picture, and there are no other objects in the picture. Why, you might ask, are these facts significant? Maybe the house is heated electrically or maybe its occupants have moved and the house is empty. Could this explain why it was drawn this way? No, unhappily, it could not.

With this picture, Kim is sending out warning signals. He is telling us that he is not thinking and feeling the way most 5-year-olds do about themselves and about the objects in their environment. We know this because he is not drawing the way most boys his age draw. The signals in Kim's drawing serve as a warning for someone to stop and pay attention. Kim may be in trouble. How to recognize some of these warning signals and how to interpret them are things we will learn in a later chapter.

This book was written for parents and teachers. While it is not designed to turn the reader into an art therapist who can expertly evaluate the drawings of children, it is meant to give you enough insight into your child's drawings to determine from them whether the child is developing normally or needs help. This can be a significant aid for parents as well as for teachers, who are in a position to see artwork produced by children in the natural course of everyday activities.

The text and children's drawings found in this book will provide you with a frame of reference. When warning signals seem to indicate a problem that requires professional attention, the book will serve as a consumer's guide, telling you when and where to find professional assistance and how to judge the qualifications of those professionals.

WHY IS ART THERAPY SO HELPFUL?

For the healthy child, art therapy is a way to chart intellectual and emotional growth. For the learning-disabled child, who often feels inadequate, acceptance of the child's artwork may be the first step in helping him or her toward self-acceptance. For the emotionally disturbed child, whose fantasies seem real, art provides a way to separate fantasy from fact.

Why should a child's art convey such significant clues?

You need only look around you for the answers. In our lifetime, visual images have become powerful rivals for words. Images inform, educate, and entertain us—they have even helped elect presidents of the United States. That art therapy has developed during this era of visual images is no mere coincidence.

The behaviors of children are given many names. The parent may call them good, bad, wild, sweet, bashful, shy, disobedient, or stubborn, whereas the art psychotherapist uses more technical terms that make reference to denial, avoidance, altruism, and resistance. No matter what terms we apply, a behavior can be a key to assessing a child's developmental well-being. Looking at a child's pictures is one method for evaluating these behaviors.

While the era of visual images was emerging, there were also great social changes. Within the past 15 years the nuclear family has split like the atom for which it was originally named. Divorce has almost become the norm, not the sad exception. This has led to a proliferation of self-help groups that offer resources not only for the harried single parent, but also for that parent's confused offspring. In our society today, more and more mothers are working outside the home, and mothers who do not work for money are sometimes regarded almost with suspicion. While once the nearby extended family of grandparents, cousins, and aunts and uncles provided additional emotional support, now these relatives are more likely to be found only at the other end of a long-distance phone call. Newspapers and television provide daily reports about battered and sexually abused children, many of whom will draw on paper what they would never be able to express in words.

As the nuclear family has been fragmented over the past 15 years, the art psychotherapist has been able to help mend some of the emotional trauma. This specialist is trained to evaluate and elicit associations from children's drawings just like those seen on classroom bulletin boards or on the doors of family refrigerators. Events, actions, and objects in a drawing represent the wishes and fears of the child who made the drawing, just as the events, actions, and objects in a dream represent the wishes and fears of the dreamer.

It may seem surprising, but the drawings of normal children all over the world show developmental progress in similar ways, despite cultural or ethnic differences. Knowledge of this expected sequence is particularly useful in evaluating the stages of your own child's development, whether it is normal and healthy or stressful emotionally or physically.

This book will cover the development of children from ages 18 months through 11 years, explaining how the pictures they draw serve as a mental "yardstick" by which to assess the state of their health and growth. We will discuss the progression of children's artistic development at different ages:

- Through age 2, children begin to scribble and discover the look and feel of using crayons or pencils on paper.

- Through age 3, children begin to outline forms within the scribbles, delighting in the discoveries of the circle and the square.

- Through ages 4 and 5, children begin to draw images with a purpose in mind and will readily explain to you what those shapes and forms mean. The sun may become a face or part of a flower. The sun's rays may become arms, legs, ears, hair, or head decorations. Ears will become large, heads will be bigger than bodies, and hats will grace those large heads. Boats, cars, and houses will be formed from squares and circles. Picture ideas will come from fantasies, environments, and stories read or told to children—

Peter will be there in the tree, figuring out how to catch that mean old wolf below.

• Finally, the child reaches the first artistic stage of sex differentiation, where "Mommy" grows breasts right on the paper and "Daddy" does not. You will learn how, at this stage, you can spot warning signs of emotional trouble, learning disabilities, and in rare instances, brain damage.

Why stop at age 11? By the age of 11 years, children have developed the skills they will use to cope with adult life. Unfortunately, by the preteen years many children also have stopped drawing. In most schools a child who has not demonstrated unusual artistic ability is not encouraged to pursue further art studies. Another deterrent is that arts programs are the last to be supported by stringent school budgets. Preadolescent energy is more likely to be channeled into physical pursuits—sports, social dancing, and group activities. Although drawings can still be revealing at this age (and even through adulthood), they now must be considered in a completely different context. That is beyond the scope of this book.

As you learn about artistic expression, you will discover that your child's art can be viewed as an open book—one that must be read carefully. Your awareness of this source of information may help you to minimize the mental stress that may lurk in the future shadows of your child's life. How well you can use this information to assist your child will be a measure of how well we have succeeded in guiding you.

Chapter 1

What Children Reveal in Their Drawings

Would you like to know when your child is happy? Sad? Excited? Frustrated? Angry? Scared? Obviously any concerned parent or anyone responsible for the care of children wants to know these things. We are always looking for clues in children's behavior or asking for verbal explanations when they do or say something that is not immediately clear to us. Yet even discovering clues and hearing verbal explanations may not make it clear. But there is a whole set of clues that most parents and teachers overlook—the clues in children's drawings.

This chapter contains drawings that flash warning signals as well as drawings that have been created by normal children. The accompanying explanations will help you to recognize the differences between these two sets of creative expressions. However, you must look with caution. A drawing may tell us what a child is feeling, but a single drawing cannot tell us the whole story. We must remind ourselves continually that although a drawing can tell us *what* is happening it will not necessarily tell us *why* it is happening. Later, you will read examples of how the art psychotherapist works to discover the *why*. You will also learn what you can do as a parent and a teacher.

SOME COMMON WARNING SIGNALS

At this point we will present some common warning signals found in children's drawings. Later, the implications of these signals will be discussed in detail.

Figure 2

There are several reasons for concern in this picture (figure 2) by 7-year-old Rafe. First, the drawing generally looks like one that normally would be produced by a younger child. Second, Rafe's lines are shaky. He seems not to have been able to stay within his own boundaries.

Another child, Arthur, at age 6, should have been able to draw recognizable objects. He *was* able to *say* what he wanted to draw, but his graphic productions tell the trained observer that he was not able to *draw* a single object that resembled his verbal descriptions.

Bobby, 3, drew at every opportunity. Every image of a face had a huge gaping mouth, and it did not matter whether the face was supposed to be a monster, his mother, or his father. A consistent form produced over

Figure 3

and over as Bobby did is a warning signal. Two examples of this repeated form are seen in figure 3.

Inconsistencies within the same picture (figure 4) demand our attention and concern. Lori, 10, has drawn one figure that is typical of a 10-year-old, yet in the same drawing the second figure and the house are so different that they could have been drawn by another child.

Figure 4

We have already discussed Kim's floating house (figure 1) and identified the elements that make it a warning signal. Kitty, 9, drew circles around floating figures (figure 5). The figures of the family members are drawn well for a 9-year-old, but isolating each member in a bubble should be viewed as a warning signal.

Figure 5

Elaine at the same age as Kitty drew the figures of her family members with complete heads and very strange and incomplete bodies. The warning signal flashes when a 9-year-old omits body parts.

Slanted images at any age need to be investigated. Rafe, 7, drew a house that appears to be falling (figure 6). Stu, 9 years old, drew himself and his "Mom" (figure 7). Like Rafe's house, the figures also look as though they are falling over.

Figure 6

Figure 7

Figure 8

The story a picture tells may be a recognizable symbol of danger. Owen, 9, has drawn a killer whale dripping blood (figure 8). It is possible that he had just seen the movie *Jaws*. But he may have a serious problem.

Once again we must emphasize that *what* is in a picture does not necessarily tell us *why*. All of these pictures flashed signals that said "check out this child." The most skilled and experienced art psychotherapist would not make a judgment based on only a drawing. Much more would need to be learned about each child before the therapist could conclude that there was a specific problem. But the parent of a young child has a context within which to try to understand the clues seen in drawings. Although these clues are not *answers,* they can lead us to ask the proper *questions*. In the chapters discussing in depth the different age groups we will return to these drawings, giving more information about each child.

SOME COMMON NORMAL INDICATORS

The following drawings and descriptions illustrate some of the skills developed by normal children at different ages.

Figure 9

The picture drawn by Gale, 9, shows us very clearly that she knew the difference between men and women (Mom and Dad) and the accurate size relationship between adults and children (figure 9).

At 4 years of age, a child should be connecting different shapes that begin to look like something recognizable. Hal has done just that (figure 10).

Figure 10

Rae, at 7, had no problem illustrating words in a way that tells us she knew what they meant. At 7 that should be a simple task (figure 11). Renee and Lewis, both 6 years old and in the same school as Rae, were also capable of accomplishing this task, which includes drawing complete figures and recognizable objects and illustrating feelings and actions like crying and jumping.

Figure 11

Letitia was 8 years old and in the second grade. Her choices of images to illustrate the words the teacher assigned show how well she could stay within her own boundaries (figure 12).

Figure 12

Figure 13

The first thing children do when they learn to hold a pencil or crayon is scribble. Joey and Hal, aged 2 and 3 years, were developing their own styles of nonverbal communication. An example of a typical scribble for this developmental period is illustrated in figure 13.

Making fine line drawings and creating designs takes time and skill. Nina, 9, was able to do this when drawing her favorite butterfly. Handling paints takes time too. Hal was only 2 when he started to use them. It was evident from his first efforts that he was not yet very adept, but at 2 he was not expected to be.

Dayna, age 4, was beginning to try to make figures by connecting the lines and circles she had mastered when she was doing a lot of scribbling. You can still see some of the scribbles in this picture (figure 14).

Becca, at 5½, was trying to tell us a story about a house, a car, the sun, and the sky (figure 15). Becca's house is firmly on the ground, telling us she was drawing normally for her age.

Figure 14

Figure 15

THE INFLUENCE OF CHANGES IN OUR SOCIETY

Children in all parts of the world begin to draw in the same way; later we will describe this process in detail. For now it is important to know that there are normal ranges of artistic development, allowing us to evaluate whether a drawing is appropriate for a particular child's age level. In making this evaluation we must also be aware of cultural influences and the ages at which children begin to include these influences in their drawings. Finally, we need to remember that our society is changing constantly, resulting in changes in normal developmental images. A very important example of this is the way television has affected our children.

When I first began practicing art therapy in the 1960s, while television was still enjoying its innocence, I learned that most children draw stick figures at about age 7. This was expected behavior, because children this age usually are not interested in differentiating between the sexes. Between 7 and 10 years, most children are interested primarily in school and playing with their peers. They learn that the stick figure is an accepted representation of the human form.

In the 1970s, changes in the stick figures became noticeable. Children between ages 7 and 9 were beginning to draw sexual characteristics on their figures, differentiating between male and female. I began to question whether these children were precocious or being exposed to adult sexual behavior. To explore this phenomenon, I contacted colleagues in other parts of the country and discovered that they were observing the same changes. We finally concluded that it was becoming natural for children to draw sexual characteristics at an earlier age than in the past because they were seeing an emphasis of female/male characteristics/differences on television—not only in the regular programming, but also in the commercials. As society continues to change, it will be more and more common to see these changes reflected in children's drawings.

THE FOUNDATIONS OF ART THERAPY

Anything created by someone—a drawing, a painting, a piece of sculpture—is a nonverbal message from the creator about the inner self and that artist's world. We have no difficulty accepting this obvious fact when we observe a painting by van Gogh or Picasso, However, we frequently suppress it when looking at the work of children, because we assume that children's pictures are "innocent"—freely expressed and totally devoid of any "hidden meaning." Acceptance of the fact that children's art expressions do have meaning is the first step toward understanding how the art therapist works. It is important to mention again that the qualified art psychotherapist always seeks additional information about the child and will not indiscriminately draw conclusions from artwork alone.

As early as 1912, psychiatrists began to recognize the value of drawings in diagnosing emotional problems. What they did not yet know was the importance of collecting information about the artist along with the drawings in order to achieve the first component of art therapy—diagnosis.

The second component of art therapy is actual treatment—the use of art to help heal emotional stress. Among art therapists, there are two schools of thought—"Art as Therapy" and "Art in Therapy." The "Art as Therapy" approach assumes that the very act of creating something artistic (and this includes music and dance) is healing. Any expression of art can be a way to obtain pleasure, release tension, or express anger. Just stop for a moment and think—do you doodle, sing in the shower, or start dancing when you hear music? If you do not, it may be because somewhere along the path of growing up you became inhibited. As we have said before and will repeat many times, all children do these things naturally.

This "Art as Therapy" approach emerged in the 1930s and 1940s, when a small group of artists began working with mental patients in hospitals and with problem children in residential treatment centers. Most of these artists were invited into these settings by administrators and psychiatrists who believed that some form of art activity would be very beneficial to these patients. It was not very long before these artists were being called art therapists. Their writings tell us how, after drawing, sculpting, or painting, some of the patients' symptoms were diminished.

The other approach—"Art in Therapy"—also emerged in the 1930s and 1940s with a different group of art therapists. These art therapists began to examine the drawings of disturbed children and adults for clues about what the patients were saying about themselves consciously and to elicit associations that would help the art therapist determine what the patients were saying about themselves unconsciously. The goal of these art therapists was very similar to the goals of psychoanalysts who encourage patients to discuss dreams and childhood memories. Many art therapists and other mental health professionals began to realize that the artist—whether the patient was a child or adult, normal or abnormal—produced images that could be likened to having dreams in a waking state. Helping the artist become aware of all the parts of the image, and of the thoughts and feelings that produced that image, was a new and provocative approach to revealing hidden feelings and thoughts. Sometimes these thoughts and feelings became available even when traditional psychotherapeutic practices had failed to disclose them. These art therapists now frequently identify themselves as art psychotherapists.

Since the early 1960s, the field of art therapy has grown rapidly. A national governing body, the American Art Therapy Association (AATA), was established in 1967, and there are now more than 2,000 registered art therapists. While an art psychotherapist may seek more information about unconscious thoughts and feelings than an art therapist, practitioners in both categories qualify for professional registration by AATA. Formal training programs are now available all over the country; in order to obtain professional standing, the AATA recommends that applicants possess an undergraduate degree with a major in the fine arts or art education and graduate training in art therapy.

As the number of art therapists/psychotherapists has grown, there have been many contributions to the literature about art therapy. These contributions have helped to sharpen our skills, broaden our scope, and develop more comprehensive training programs. Years of experience have also led us to search continually for new ways to use our knowledge and skills and new ways to describe to others in related professions how to "hear" what we see.

A few art therapists continue to adhere to either the "Art as Therapy" or the "Art in Therapy" approach. Many more have become sensitive to the fact that some people benefit more from one approach than from the other, and more often mix the two approaches. The qualified art therapist today is able to provide the best means of artistic expression for a particular patient, regardless of which approach is recommended.

Art therapists have learned to blend art skills with different psychological theories, and many are members of treatment teams including psychiatrists, psychologists, social workers, teachers, nurses, and other physicians. Sometimes the art therapist is responsible only for conducting an evaluation and imparting information about the evaluation to others who are directing a course of intervention or treatment. At other times art therapists actually direct and conduct the intervention or treatment based on conclusions reached jointly with other mental health professionals.

The first small group of art therapists evolved an identity for their specialty by working with psychiatrists in hospital settings for very disturbed mental patients and residential schools for problem children. Today, art therapists work in public and private schools with normal, abnormal, and handicapped children, and in prisons, inpatient units in hospitals, outpatient clinics, day-care centers, and nursing homes. Art therapists help prepare children for surgery and other hospital procedures, work with patients receiving dialysis for kidney disease, and provide counseling for children and adults faced with the physical and mental trauma of terminal illness. In all of these situations the artistic expression provides another way for that person to cope with the illness and to express feelings that might otherwise remain hidden.

Some art therapists are in private practice, some are family therapists, and some are licensed professionals in other areas of mental health. Regardless of career direction, the crucial qualification of the successful art therapist is the individual ability to work creatively to mesh art skills with an in-depth knowledge of nonverbal communication.

Now that you know something about the history of art therapy, we can discuss how to help you help your child.

CREATIVE EXPRESSION THROUGH ART

The artist creates order out of disorder. This disorder may be something the artist feels inside or something chaotic perceived in the environment. Whatever the source, the artistic image that emerges is one that is orderly and said to be "universally appealing." This does not mean that everyone who looks at a given work of art will like it. It does imply that the final product disguises the artist's personal thoughts and feelings so that the viewer will relate to the subject matter and not to the person of the artist. Not every artist is always totally successful in accomplishing this. We have all seen famous works of art and wondered what the artist was thinking. The concept of universal appeal is a simplification of the basic criteria for identifying a work of art. If we can begin to understand how the artist, through the creative process, transforms personal chaotic feelings and ideas into order, we can begin to understand how children naturally use drawings to organize the multitude of new experiences they encounter as they grow and create a sense of balance within themselves.

The very disturbed mental patient often has a need to draw. One manifestation of mental illness is that the person feels helpless and longs to be a child again—to be coddled and protected. It is the childlike quality in the disturbed adult that elicits spontaneous drawings. These patients, too, are making order out of chaos, but it is a personal chaos and the images are often childlike, fragmented, and even bizarre. The meaning is known only to the person who produces the art. The subject matter is not drawn in a way that holds universal appeal as do the images produced by the professional artist.

Children seem to have a need to draw. Like the artist and the mental patient, children will communicate nonverbally whenever given the opportunity. Normally, a child will take to paper and crayon like a duck to water. Most of us have forgotten our earliest years, but everyone who has been involved in caring for a small child knows that each new experience and sensation confronting the child is unsettling, whether the immediate response is one of distress or pleasure. Putting that sensation or experience on paper, changing it, adding to it, crossing it out, and connecting it to known objects and events, all are ways of organizing and reorganizing what is new with what is already known. This is one way of mastering the process of growing up.

I have led you from the artist to the patient to the child, in order to remind you that the child in all of us was once a budding artist. The practicing artist is doing professionally what we all did so naturally as children whenever given the opportunity. A few more examples from the world around us might be helpful, but before sharing these with you, I want to dispel a myth. Sometime in your life you may have heard people say something like "artists are crazy." Whether you believed it or not, in order to appreciate the art in art therapy and the role of the creative process in mental health, this myth must be dispelled. A truly disturbed—even though talented—artist is no more able to make order out of chaos and create an image that disguises personal torment than is a mentally disturbed person who is not artistically talented. This statement can be supported by the example of Vincent van Gogh, an artist who has been described by some as "that crazy artist who cut off his ear." His biographers, however, tell us that when van Gogh was seriously mentally disturbed he did not want to paint. Although he spent the last year of his life in a mental hospital, most of the paintings produced during that year were created when he was lucid and in touch with reality. Looking at van Gogh's works in chronological order over that last year of his life, one can sadly see the deterioration of this man's artistic ability.

Pablo Picasso, on the other hand, did not suffer periods of personal torment that prevented him from creating. But we know his artwork was influenced and affected by personal and world events. *Guernica,* one of Picasso's most famous paintings, depicts his personal feelings about war; his incredible talent and mental stability turned these feelings into an artistic, nonverbal statement that can be understood by anyone who sees this expressive, dramatic painting.

Every day some of us see a form of art that is one way some teenagers try to make order out of their chaotic lives—graffiti. We generally regard this as a form of vandalism. In some large metropolitan cities, gangs of teenagers from low-income families have been encouraged and supervised to productively apply graffiti, and compete with each other to create beautiful designs. Another current and important teenage expression, although not graphic production, is breakdancing. Children from all walks of life can be seen struggling to master intricate gyrations—they are literally "breaking out" in dance.

The budding artist that was a part of all of us when we were children was not always allowed to continue to express itself freely and creatively. Children need to organize their feelings and thoughts as they develop, and one way to do this is through creative expression.

NORMAL STAGES/SEQUENCES OF ARTISTIC DEVELOPMENT

The rest of this chapter will summarize what can be expected from a child at each major stage of artistic development, with examples of typical drawings for each stage/sequence. Then chapters 4 through 7 will cover these periods of development in greater detail. The relationship among emotional development, intellectual development, and creative expression charted by the growing child through artworks will become clearer for you as we continue to explore the wonderful world of children's pictures. Before learning about normal stages of development, however, you should know that many art psychotherapists and psychologists do not totally accept the concept of *stages of development*.

A stage, in psychological terms, generally implies that a period of development has a definite beginning and ending. When discussing children, however, experience teaches us that not all children develop at the same pace. This does not mean that the slower child is less bright or less skilled, but only that for some reason this child is traveling along the path of development differently from most children. We also know that certain skills must be mastered before a child can learn a new task. This is particularly true in developing skills in drawing, and I believe that it is also true in intellectual development. As children are learning new skills, they are still practicing and perfecting skills learned previously. Therefore, rather than use the term *stage*, I will use the term *stage/sequence*. Ages given for each period will be meant only as general guidelines; a developmentally normal child may perform certain skills a little earlier or later with no cause for concern.

Babble-Scribble Stage/Sequence: Around 18 months to 2½ years

Between 18 months and 2½ years, children are developing the ability to grasp objects and move them around. Given paper and crayon, they will delight in creating lines of different lengths and seeing them emerge in different directions. There is no apparent rhyme or reason to these early scribblings, just the sheer joy in the movement and the image. As the child gains greater body control, the lines begin to take form. A child may name an object if prompted by an adult.

Doug was 2 years 1 month old when he drew figure 16, and Hal a little past 2 when he made figure 17.

Figure 16

Figure 17

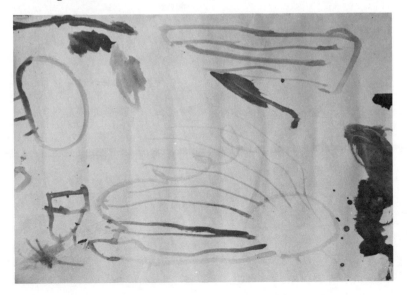

Word-Shape Stage/Sequence: Around 2½ to 4 years

At the Word-Shape Stage/Sequence the child begins to outline forms within the scribbles. Just as words are expressed randomly at first, shapes appear randomly. Very gradually these shapes become familiar circles and squares. Children begin to draw with a plan in mind; depending on the amount and variety of stimulation in the environment and the availability of materials, they will produce drawings that are more or less complex. They will experiment with combining different shapes, but often will not know what they are drawing until the work is finished. If asked, they will tell a story about their drawing.

Hal was 3 years old and experimenting with paints. He also had discovered he could combine circles with lines. When asked, he said one of his creations was a "crawling bug" and another "flowers" (figure 18).

Figure 18

Indira and Gamal, both 3-year-old children from India, experimented with paints in the same way as their American counterparts. Although they did not say what they had created, their paintings were very similar to Hal's productions.

Sentence-Picture Stage/Sequence: Around 4 to 7 years

At ages 4 to 7, children learn to complete simple sentences and draw pictures that tell a simple story. During this time they become more aware of and influenced by their culture and environment.

Age 4   Scott has mastered the ability to draw a circle and to connect circles and lines to create a facelike image (figure 19). Bobby, also 4, was able to combine lines, scribbles, and circles to create different peoplelike images.

Figure 19

Age 5 Scott's mastery of all the things he had learned before helped him to create more complete figures with all the body parts and even (scribble) hair. Scott's growing skills are described and illustrated below.

Age 6 Scott and Lilly have moved into what is known as the pictorial stage. Scott combined his knowledge of shapes and lines to draw a picture of a house, a tree, and a person (figure 20). Lilly was more interested in using her knowledge and skill at this time to draw a sun, a huge flower, and a girl with a big bow in her hair (figure 21). We expect to see all the body parts around this time, but it is not unusual for them to be distorted. One leg bigger than the other is not surprising and may even be expected; we will explain why in chapter 6.

Figure 20

Figure 21

Fact-Fantasy Stage/Sequence: Around 7 to 11 years

By this age children have acquired many facts about the important people in their environment and have developed fantasies about their world. They should be able to draw realistically and to improve on this skill continually. Their drawings should reflect their feelings, thoughts, and fantasies prompted by their surroundings. Drawings provide an appropriate and natural way for children in this age group to deal with the newness of school and peer interactions.

Figure 22

Age 7 Brad's illustrations all show his rich combinations of reality and fantasy, especially his picture (figure 22) of the teacher behind the desk shouting, "NO!" Leah, also 7, was able to use her own experiences to show the teacher what words meant to her. She illustrated a little girl "jumping" rope, a child doing "work" at her desk, and a person "crying."

Age 7½ Scott did not like snowmen, and one way to deal with that was to make the snowman a robot that he could control. He drew a white robot marching down snow-covered hills.

Age 8   Nina's and Tillie's pieces of art show the ability to handle pencil and crayon, draw realistically, and use imagination to create original responses to a second-grade assignment. Their choices of examples to illustrate the words reflect familiar things in their environment. An example of this is seen in figure 23, one of Nina's drawings.

Figure 23

Age 9 to 10   Randy, age 9, could represent his ideas so well by now that he enjoyed drawing fanciful images to illustrate those ideas (figure 24). Sue, 10, was able to draw people of all different ages realistically enough for us to recognize everyone in her "nice" family portrait; she also was able to make a clear distinction between males and females. Herb, 9½, drew war scenes, which are very typical for boys this age.

Figure 24

These examples illustrate the most common kinds of images we see sequentially in drawings of children who are growing normally. The children who produced these drawings are all physically well, functioning in the appropriate school grade for their age. This small sampling represents children from different socioeconomic groups, different religions, different races, and different parts of the world.

This brief outline of the important stages/sequences of growth includes only normal developmental sequences.

Because each child is unique and each child grows at his or her own pace, manifestations of abnormal development at any stage/sequence cannot be defined easily without considering both the child's physical history from birth and the environment at home and school at the time we see those warning signals.

There is a definite relationship between intelligence and artistic expression. A child cannot draw an object before being able to identify it intellectually. Normal intellectual development provides the child with the skills necessary to draw more recognizable objects. As the child learns more, drawings of objects become more detailed. Drawings are one way to measure intellectual development.

The next chapters, which discuss each age group, will demonstrate how a knowledge of normal stages/sequences of development helps us to determine whether a child is facing developmental stresses normal for that age or whether the danger signals we see mean far more serious problems.

Chapter 2
What You Can Learn from What I Do

As a member of the helping professions, I know too well that most people do not seek help until there is a serious problem. Even then the tendency is to deny that there is a problem until, for whatever reason, dealing with it can no longer be avoided. This kind of denial is normal, but a delay in getting help frequently makes the problem greater. It is not easy to admit that we may need outside help in raising our children.

Sometimes, however, outside help can reassure us that the warning signals in a child's drawings do not indicate a problem that needs intervention. Rather, we may learn that the child has naturally found a way to deal with a problem. The case of young Bobby illustrates this point.

Very often, when people learn that I am an art therapist, they will try to test me with a drawing. This occurred a few years ago, when my husband and I met Bobby's grandparents at a resort. After we had known each other for a while and had exchanged the usual bits of information about ourselves and our families, they asked if I would look at some drawings that their 4-year-old grandson had produced. He loved to draw, and they just wanted to know whether he was drawing as other 4-year-olds drew. After seeing a number of drawings I realized that this little boy had a real problem. You have already seen an example of

Bobby's pictures—figure 3. In that drawing, produced when he was 3, a huge gaping mouth was included in the images of a face; in fact this was true of every face he drew. I truthfully told his grandparents that his drawings were like those of other children his age, but that the gaping mouth was a warning signal. I asked whether Bobby was having a problem with his teeth or had sustained an injury to his mouth. The grandparents told me that Bobby had been born with a cleft palate and was in the process of reconstructive surgery.

The most impressive aspect of Bobby's natural creativity is that we can see how his drawings served to help him master and cope with this very real trauma. As surgery was completed and Bobby had more time to think about other things like school and friends, the faces began to show more realistic proportions. The gaping mouth appeared only occasionally. A "rabbit with whiskers," produced when Bobby was 3 years 2 months, and a robotlike face, drawn when he was 4, still show elaboration of detail around the mouth. Figure 25, drawn at age 4, shows that Bobby was starting to combine shapes and lines to create a variety of images and even to begin to tell a story. Looking through

Figure 25

Figure 26

his drawings, we can still see a representation of trauma during his fifth year (figure 26). At 6, he created a design out of a star and included the members of his family (figure 27). There is now no evidence of the gaping mouth.

Figure 27

Recently, while visiting his grandparents, Bobby brought me a drawing he had just completed. This showed what appeared to be a colorful design with two distinctly separate parts. When the picture was turned to the right, the bottom form looked like a gaping mouth with teeth. Before I asked, his grandmother told me Bobby was having trouble with a new tooth. What was so interesting was that this trouble was now relegated to only half of the picture rather than dominating it.

In his early pictures, Bobby flashed warning signals by repeating a specific image over and over. These drawings tell us that he needed to master his thoughts and feelings about the physical trauma he was experiencing; drawing the image of a mouth over and over provided a way to do that. Bobby's drawings also tell us when that need began to lessen naturally. His most recent drawing tells us he can have a problem, even one connected with his mouth, without its becoming the most important thing in his life. Now he can pay attention to other things at the same time. Bobby is lucky. His parents, grandparents, and teachers encourage him to express himself and express some of his growing pains on paper. If we take time to look, Bobby will always tell us how he is progressing. At age 8 he is progressing very well.

HOW THE ART PSYCHOTHERAPIST WORKS

Lori was an above-average student in school and had no observable problems. At 10 she was the youngest of four children, with three older brothers aged 14, 16, and 18. Her parents had been receiving marriage counseling for about six months, and I had been supervising their cotherapists, who were student interns in a family therapy program. When the parents expressed concern about one son I requested an evaluation of the whole family. The parents agreed to participate with their children in a verbal interview by a senior family therapist, as well as in an art therapy family evaluation that I conducted, and in a movement therapy assessment. The entire evaluation provided information that had remained hidden until that time, and allowed us to redirect the focus and course of the parents' therapy sessions. Let us look at what Lori told us.

In the art therapy evaluation Lori and her family were directed to draw two pictures. The first was to be "anything you want to draw." Lori drew a picture (figure 28) she called "first in line" and said it was "someone who had been first in line, got burned, and was in the hospital." The person to the right of the figure in bed was a nurse who was also "burned" when she came to help the patient. The second picture Lori drew was in response to the request to draw a "family picture" (figure 4). Both of these drawings told us that she was feeling a lot of stress.

Figure 28

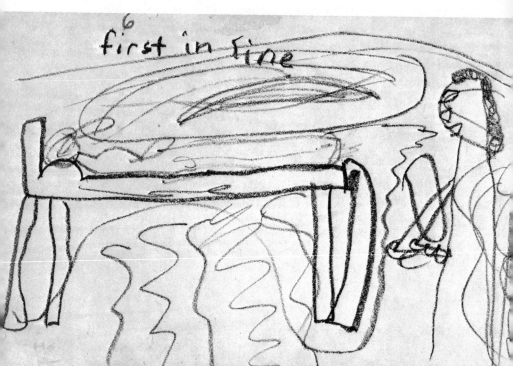

We knew that Lori was bright because she was able to represent one figure so well in the family picture. The inconsistencies in the way she drew other objects, the use of much immature scribbling, the subject matter of someone who was first in line and getting burned, and the preoccupation with trash, all communicated to us that she was feeling very disorganized. Lori's being intelligent made it possible for us to help her connect the disorganization in her drawings to the disorder she felt at home. Her parents had insisted that she was too young to know that they were having marital problems. In fact, this child knew more about what was going on than did her brothers. Lori, who had been trying to maintain order at home by pretending she did not know about her parents' problems, was finally able to release her anxieties on paper with the support of the three therapists. When we explained to her parents what Lori was communicating, they were able to use the guidance of the therapists to reestablish a sense of order and security in their house for all of the children, especially Lori.

Lori's warning signals told us she was feeling considerable emotional stress. In this case, information obtained from the entire family in an extensive evaluation procedure told us that the parents were not fully aware of their children's feelings. When the drawings served as documentation for those feelings, they could no longer be denied.

Two children, Rafe, 7, and Arthur, 6, were mentioned in chapter 1. Each showed examples of warning signals (see Rafe's picture, figure 2). Both of these boys were students in a school for learning-disabled children. They had difficulty in closing shapes, could not draw recognizable objects, drew slanted forms, and repeated forms and lines over and over. These are all indications of a learning disorder that includes a perceptual problem. The school art therapist told us how she worked in that setting with learning-disabled children.

Apparently Arthur's problems were not as severe as Rafe's. With assistance, Arthur could copy shapes. However, it was decided that both boys should be taught basic shapes such as squares and circles and should be guided through early developmental drawing sequences. They would be helped to master one sequence before they were introduced to the next. Over a period of several school years they were given special projects such as shapes to feel and trace. Some of these tasks emerged from discussions with their classroom teacher; everyone working with these children was using a consistent approach to helping them learn. Rafe's progress is shown in figure 29. Arthur's progress is shown in figure 30.

The relationship between perceptual skills and reading skills is critical, and an art therapist can be a particularly useful member of the team in a school for learning-disabled children. Knowledge of intellectual and emotional development is necessary to work with impaired children,

Figure 29

Figure 30

who can learn, through art, to express feelings related to their problems.

A learning-disabled child may be average or even above-average in intelligence. Sometimes drawings are our first clues to a child's intelligence, because these children cannot learn through traditional classroom methods. In children, the diagnosis of mental retardation, emotional disturbance, or learning disability is made on the basis of observation of some form of behavior. Often it is very difficult to test these children with traditional psychological procedures.

A number of years ago I was serving as a consultant to a local school in which some of our art therapy students were working with a class of emotionally disturbed children. At the monthly team meetings, which included the classroom teacher, the school psychologist, the school counselor, the school principal, a representative from the special education department of the board of education, and me, we discussed a 7-year-old boy. He had temper tantrums in the classroom and was sometimes unmanageable. We were told that his father was alcoholic and that both his mother and father seemed to have poor parenting skills. However, someone familiar with the family reported that this child was well cared for, was dressed very neatly, and was escorted to the school bus each morning. Nevertheless, the consensus was that he had to be disturbed because of the family history. In these meetings I was usually asked to review whatever drawings were available, and it was assumed that I would confirm the diagnosis. This was not the case, however. The child's drawings told me that he was having difficulty expressing himself in an organized fashion and that he had not mastered early developmental sequences. It was possible that this seemingly bright child might be frustrated because he could not learn the way other children did and that the temper tantrums were an expression of this frustration. Further psychological testing for a perceptual problem confirmed what we saw in the drawings. This child was removed from the class for emotionally disturbed children and was placed in a class for learning-disabled children, where appropriate instruction was available. Unfortunately, conclusive judgments are too often made on insufficient information and/or false assumptions. I could not keep the drawings produced by this child, but the next series of drawings reflects a similar situation.

I spent a month working in a preschool in the United Kingdom. The school has a well-qualified staff and is associated with a training center of psychologists that provides consultation if needed. Most of the children in this nursery school are from single-parent families or from homes in which both parents are employed. Only under unusual circumstances and by special recommendation does the school accept children who are known to have serious emotional problems. The children are admitted as young as 3 if they are toilet-trained. Community law requires that by age 5 all children are enrolled in a regular accredited school setting.

During the time I was at the school, problems were diagnosed in three of the ten children. I was *not* there officially as an art psychotherapist. My plan was to work with "normal" preschoolers in art activities, collecting their drawings for further study. The staff was very cooperative, introducing me as an "art lady" and allowing me the freedom to engage the children in drawing or painting during indoor play. The staff, aware of my training and experience, invited me to join the weekly staff meetings.

Michael was 4 years 10 months old when I arrived at the school, and plans were being made for his entrance into a regular school. He was very articulate, but seemed to be aware that he should be able to do certain things better than he did. For example, he could not do puzzles easily unless someone pointed out the colors of the pieces and helped him match them to the picture on the cover of the puzzle box. Michael's frustration over such situations frequently led to explosive behavior. The teachers had assumed that Michael's behavior resulted from his home environment, which was fraught with marital discord. There had been a number of separations and reconciliations between his parents, and at this time his father had been absent from the home for a year. The assumption that Michael's problems reflected his home situation seemed to be well founded, and I expected to see evidence of this in Michael's drawings.

What I saw in the first drawing Michael made for me was a very bizarre image of a house with a staircase. The picture was far below a 4- to 5-year-old developmental level, and the shaky lines and slant to the house led me to question whether Michael might have a perceptual problem caused by minimal brain dysfunction. Michael had been given a standard intelligence test several months earlier, and his emotional problems had been considered when grading this test. The routine evaluations conducted at the school did not include more involved testing that could discern the presence of minimal brain dysfunction.

Figure 31   Figure 32

To save time, I was asked to do an art therapy evaluation to determine whether there was consistent evidence of the problem I suspected. Knowing Michael's frustration level, I gave him only three tasks. For the usual art therapy evaluation I would use at least five tasks, and possibly six, a standard practice among most trained art therapists.

At my direction, Michael did three drawings—a free drawing that he said was a car (figure 31), a house that looked like a scribble in a rectangle, and a person who he said was a "man who was cross" (figure 32). Throughout the evaluation process, Michael was aware that the drawings did not look like what he said they were, and he needed much encouragement to complete them. The drawings confirmed my original suspicions and the consulting psychologist concurred. Michael's emotional problems were also evident, particularly in a drawing of his family that is discussed in chapter 6. The positive result of this evaluation was that Michael's mother, who was undergoing therapy, was able to cope with her own personal stress and do something to help her son. She made arrangements for him to receive tutoring in a specialized school program and to meet a therapist once a week. It is always risky to try to predict the results of any intervention, but it is believed that Michael will do well if this kind of support from mother and school continues.

By contrast let us consider Brian, who was 4 years 3 months old when he drew a cement truck (figure 33) and "Brian crying" (figure 34). The drawing of the cement truck is very advanced for a child of this age, telling us that Brian is very bright. His intellectual development, as evidenced by the drawing, is closer to a 6-year-old's than to a 4-year-old's. His truck sits on the ground and is drawn very much like a toy truck he used in play, but that toy was not in sight when he drew this picture.

Figure 33

Figure 34

Brian's drawing of himself tells another story. He does not see himself as a whole person and tearfully communicates his fear that he will never be complete. This same self-image was repeated in many drawings. This startling difference between Brian's drawing of an object in his environment and a drawing of himself tells us that intellectually he can represent an object in his environment when he chooses, but that he has a great deal of difficulty reflecting a normal self-image in his drawings. This kind of difference between two developmental paths, intellectual and emotional, at this early age, is a serious warning signal that Brian will not be able to adjust to school and peer relationships. He was not playing well with other children in the nursery school, and his behavior was often unpredictable and strange. In this situation, I concurred with other members of the staff that he was a very disturbed child who would probably require psychotherapy for years. I also learned that Brian's mother was very disturbed and that an effort was being made to provide treatment for her and her son.

One of the advantages in serving as a consultant to other therapists who have drawings produced by their patients or clients is that sometimes I am permitted to discuss these drawings in my writings. Jenny's two drawings came to me in this manner. Her therapist is a psychologist and registered music therapist. A well-trained clinician who knows that all children like to draw, she encourages creative expression in a variety of media. Jenny drew a self-portrait (figure 35) at age 8 shortly after she was referred for therapy. The way she drew this figure indicates that she was able to represent people on an intellectual and artistic level appropriate for her age. The image suggests fear and anger. We have learned that when children are abused they often draw themselves in very aggressive images, not unlike the person they perceive as the abuser. There were some concern in this case that Jenny was abused and was drawing herself like her mother. The figure is floating and filled in with very agitated lines.

Figure 35

Figure 36

A year later, Jenny spontaneously drew another portrait of herself (figure 36); her therapist was struck by similarities and differences between these two images. In the more recent picture, Jenny is clearly on the ground, the fierce mouth is replaced by a smile, feminine eyelashes and flying pigtails replace the glaring eyes and jagged hair, and the upraised arms support a jump rope. The second drawing clearly documents that Jenny was not feeling as angry and afraid as she had been a year before. This new drawing supports what Jenny's therapist noted in her behavior—she was a much calmer, happier child who was beginning to be able to function in a much healthier way in school and at home.

Sometimes I am not able to keep the pictures I have evaluated. Such was the case with a drawing brought to me by police investigating a series of murders. It seemed that one of the victims, a young teenager and a relative of the murderer, had drawn a sad and disturbing picture of a little boy in a cage calling for help. He gave the picture to his teacher, who did not know what to do with it, but kept it. When the police questioned people who knew the murder victims, the teacher showed them the picture, produced months before the child was killed. *He* was calling for help, but the teacher did not see what he was saying. It is impossible to say that if the teacher had known this was really a cry for help she could have prevented the child's murder. But we *can* say that we cannot afford to neglect what children draw. More and more the courts are paying attention. I am now being asked to evaluate children and parents in custody cases, with drawings submitted as evidence on behalf of the children's interests. In addition, a growing awareness of the value of nonverbal communication in drawings has led to my being called to the courtroom as an expert witness in criminal cases. Similar instances have occurred with colleagues throughout the country.

Chapter 3

How to Inspire Creative Expression

The preceding chapters provided clues to help you recognize in children's drawings some indicators of danger signals and some indicators of normal intellectual and emotional development. But these clues are useful only if children are encouraged to express themselves freely. This chapter offers recommendations to help *you* create an atmosphere in which this free expression can occur. We will suggest what kinds of media should be available at various ages and what you can do to stimulate a child's natural creative expression. We will also discuss what *not* to do—things parents and teachers do and say that can inhibit this expression and make children self-conscious about their artistic endeavors.

The first step in dealing with any child's problem is recognition of the problem itself. The next step is the attempt to define the problem by examining home and school relationships. Once the problem has been defined, proper help can be obtained. This chapter offers guidance in selecting qualified help.

ENCOURAGING CREATIVITY IN CHILDREN

The word *sublimation* is familiar to most of us. However, the meaning of this word is often disputed by mental health professionals and is frequently misused. Most psychologists accept a definition of sublimation as the ability to obtain pleasure in a socially acceptable way. This explanation of sublimation relates closely to the creative process. An example of sublimation is the artist who has learned to repress and channel the normal infantile desire to smear, into a socially acceptable activity such as painting or sculpturing.

Sublimation is considered a normal function of the healthy individual—a capacity present in all of us from birth. Therefore, sublimation is not only found in the artist. As an example, a child who is especially curious, destroying every toy in an effort to discover how it works, may sublimate this aggressive urge by pursuing a career as a research scientist—discovering why or how things work as they do.

There are many other examples of sublimation. What we need to understand for the purpose of this book is why, if we are all born with this capacity, some people seem to have it while others do not. To our knowledge, this ability to find alternate acceptable ways to gratify our most primitive wishes needs to be nurtured at an early age.

There are specific developmental tasks that must be achieved before a child can take crayon in hand and begin to learn the fun of making images on paper. These will be discussed in detail in the next chapter. For now we will consider the kind of environment that is necessary in order for children to begin creating.

First, drawing should take place in a safe area in which the child can explore art materials. The very young child should be able to move freely. Attention spans are short in these early years, and we must remember that the child may lose interest in something in a very brief period of time.

When the child is a little older, the "art area" should allow for spilling, cutting, or pasting. This need not be an area devoted exclusively to the child—it can be the kitchen table, the basement floor, or the outside porch. A good place is *any* place that provides the freedom to use the art materials in an unrestricted and individual way.

Regardless of the age of the child, production should be encouraged and the artworks valued, respecting the child's wishes about what happens to those art productions. This is not to say that they must be displayed in areas that are not acceptable to the rest of the family. However, there should be a place to show them and a place to store them. This is a way to help children begin to respect the property rights of others. For the same reason, very young siblings should be allowed to have their own sets of materials and their own space.

I know too well how difficult it is for the teacher, whether in a nursery school, elementary school, or junior high school, to provide individual freedom of artistic expression in a classroom of twenty or more children. Whatever the physical restrictions, however, teachers are responsible for helping students achieve many goals. They will demonstrate how to use various media and will help students learn to draw objects in the environment, so that the images produced are aesthetically pleasing. All of these goals are necessary steps in the learning process. Every new task a child masters provides skills that can be applied to a variety of other learning tasks. But children should not be expected to complete all assignments in the same "cookie cutter" way. I remember one first-grade student who decided to make her tree trunk purple and the leaves brown. Although the student teacher had no special training in art or art therapy, she did know that individual expression was to be encouraged, and she fortunately responded to this image with the same enthusiasm she showed when looking at more realistically colored trees.

Art therapists are taught the value of individual expression. An artist who consulted me for psychotherapy was completing his education for certification as an art teacher. Several years later at a social gathering I met a woman who told me how pleased she was with her son's art teacher in junior high school. When she mentioned him by name, I realized he was my former patient. The woman described how he made the weekly art class an exciting event for the children by providing a variety of materials such as pieces of cloth, wood, and shells, in addition to paints and clay. The children were invited to create whatever they wanted either individually or working with other classmates. Special help was provided if students were unfamiliar with certain supplies. Each piece of art produced by his students was accepted by this teacher as a unique and special creation. When I called to report the nice things I had been told about his teaching methods, he said that his experience in art therapy had made him realize how valuable it was to encourage the creative process rather than emphasize the final art product.

Not all art teachers can be or should be art therapists, but all teachers should provide a climate for individual expression. Speaking with teachers at conferences over the years, I know that more and more teachers are becoming aware of this need. They are working very hard to change rigid approaches to teaching art, such as requiring everyone in a class to produce the same image in the same way. Art teachers and art therapists have established task forces in which representatives from each group share ideas on how to help children grow through art expression. Teachers and art therapists are also defining their individual roles and responsibilities in the process.

A favorable environment is the first element necessary for free expression. The second is providing the tools to create that expression.

Children can learn to express themselves at a very early age with any materials available. Infants and toddlers have an instinctive desire to play with food, mud, and sand simply because they enjoy the feel of these elements in their environment and derive pleasure from the newly gained control over body movement. It is obvious that by the age of around 18 months to 2 years the child recognizes simple commands, such as the meaning of *no*. When the toddler can understand such simple directions and is able to grasp small objects as well as control arm movement, it is time to provide crayons and paper.

Big fat crayons are probably best in the beginning, as these can be managed easily by small hands. Any inexpensive paper is fine. Large pads are good, but you can use almost any kind of paper available around the house, so long as one side of it is blank. The only caution is to be sure that any coloring on the paper is safe. Even toddlers sometimes enjoy crumpling and tasting the paper as much as coloring on it. They may also want to taste the crayons, just as they may have tasted sand or mud. When children are this young, you need to supervise and show them how these new objects should be handled. Sit down on the floor and scribble—yes, *scribble*. Watching you is the beginning of imitating and learning how to be a grown-up person.

If a child has no physical impairments, dexterity will naturally increase. Later you may want to teach the child how to cut with blunt scissors. Construction paper is wonderful for this purpose. Children will let you know when they are ready to try new and more complicated art supplies.

Paint can be introduced as early as 3 years of age. Large jars of tempera paint and wide brushes can be purchased at a hobby or toy shop. Be sure to read labels when you buy paint or colored pencils, avoiding any material that contains lead. Swallowing of any lead-based art materials can lead to brain damage. Be sure that your child is safe from this readily avoidable catastrophe. You should also be aware that so-called lead pencils contain not lead, but graphite, a form of carbon. It is not recommended that children eat this, but it is not harmful in small quantities.

Some toddlers who are still struggling with toilet training may wish to avoid the messiness of paints; this is not unusual. There is no rush. Make paints available when you feel the child is ready. Because tempera is a water-based paint, it washes off easily. Demonstrate this to the child and explain that it is okay to be messy and have fun. Toddlers generally enjoy finger painting, delighting in creating designs from this wonderful smeary substance. However, I do not encourage older children or adults to use this medium. Finger paints encourage smearing like a small child. While the use of finger paints is a step forward in art for the toddler, it is a step backward for the older child or adult. We need to help children advance by developing controls, not by regressing and losing them.

I like to illustrate the importance of maintaining control by describing an interesting phenomenon that I have observed repeatedly when introducing art therapy to student nurses and medical students. I ask these students to do a free drawing, and I provide paper, crayons, and colored pencils. Like most adults, these students have not drawn since grade school and feel very intimidated initially. Many of them invariably produce designs by outlining shapes and filling in the outlines. This is something children learn to do early in their school years. Outlining the shapes provides control; filling in is reminiscent of scribbling. The response of these students is understandable. I am asking them to do something they consider childish. Discussion of this process is effective in helping these students develop some appreciation for art therapy. If they had been offered finger paints, they could not have established their own controls and I would have done them a disservice by inviting more regression, and perhaps even causing embarrassment.

The child's school environment can be an important factor in creative expression. Children in nursery school often learn things more quickly than they might at home.

This setting provides the added incentive of doing what the other children are doing. In nursery school there may also be a shortage of teachers or aides to help the pre-schooler test new experiences. Both teachers and parents should be aware of each child's progress, assessing whether it is consistent with that of other children and appropriate for the child's age level.

Going to school for the first time should open new vistas for the child who has been encouraged to be creative. New ideas, and perhaps new materials, will be introduced in the classroom and in peer activities. Parents should show an interest in new creative projects and encourage children to continue to create at home. Both parents and teachers should be aware of what children are saying in their art-work.

Stimulating creativity in your children requires using your own creative resources. There is no need to buy elaborate art supplies; many things around the house can be used. All of us who have "made art" with children or worked where there were limited funds for art supplies have learned to improvise with whatever was available. Books purchased or borrowed from the library can help you think of new ideas.

The message to be communicated is that parents and teachers can offer an environment that will stimulate the creativity of the children in their care. It is *not* important to run out and buy the very best art supplies. It *is* important to show the child that you are interested in the artwork, no matter what the subject matter and no matter what materials have been selected for artistic expression.

The message about the importance of stimulating creativity is emphasized in the following examples of parent/child interactions. The lessons to be learned apply to any form of creative expression.

Lynne, age 6, loved to use her mother's paintbrushes. Lynne's mother, Mrs. R, was an artist who conducted private art classes in a studio in her home. Mrs. R's students' work and art supplies were kept in a special closet, and Lynne knew she was allowed to use only those materials that were not in the closet. It was not unusual for Lynne to entertain herself by painting alone for hours.

On one such day Lynne discovered a canvas board with interesting colors and shapes on it on an easel. She decided to enhance these with her own designs. When Lynne's mother entered the studio to see what her daughter was painting, she realized too late that she had neglected to put one of her students' paintings in the closet. This painting was now almost totally obliterated by Lynne's creations. Mrs. R had to admit she alone was responsible for the destruction of her student's artwork because she had left it on the easel. To punish the child would have been unfair.

Lynne's mother acknowledged her own carelessness and asked Lynne to check with her in the future before painting on any surface that had some imagery on it. At the same time she praised her daughter's creativity so this experience would not inhibit Lynne's interest in painting. By owning her responsibility for this disaster and explaining the situation to Lynne and her student, Mrs. R helped both children learn it was okay to make mistakes but that people must also take responsibility for their actions.

Nine-year-old Evan was very involved in "Dungeons and Dragons," a fantasy adventure game. Evan was very talented artistically, drawing his own characters and creating adventures for them. His father enjoyed miniature train sets and decided that he and Evan should build a train platform. Evan did not agree. He wanted to spend the time building a castle for his "Dungeons and Dragons" characters. Evan's father was very disappointed; he thought sharing a creative activity with his son would be a special experience for them both. His assumption was correct, but the experience had to be one that interested Evan. Suppressing his own disappointment, the father told

Evan that he would be very glad to help with the castle. Together they shopped for necessary art supplies, and the father was available whenever Evan needed help. Evan's mother suggested that space in Evan's bedroom could be used to build the castle, and she offered praise as the project progressed. Evan's younger brother was told that he could watch but not touch. It is not always easy to have our children reject our interests, but Evan's father knew that, in this instance, favoring his son's interests over his own would be more productive.

BARRIERS TO CREATIVE EXPRESSION

There are many things done unwittingly by parents and teachers that result in the stifling of a child's creativity. Parents and teachers must be sensitive to the limits of a small child's curiosity and naturally short attention span. While you may have planned a half hour to "scribble" with the child, the child may have had enough after ten minutes.

We all want to demonstrate to ourselves and to others the intelligence of children. Drawing lends itself so well to identifying objects and colors that adults strain to find a recognizable object in those early shapes within shapes; when they see something that looks familiar they promptly name it. Try to refrain from doing this. Instead, ask your child to tell you a story about the picture. Until age 4 most children do not decide what they are drawing until they have finished, and even then they may not want to tell you. If you insist, they will agree with what you say, but you have made that drawing yours, not your child's. We must not judge children's art productions from our own realistic perspective.

Sometimes, in an effort to please, a parent or teacher may consent to a child's request and later regret giving this consent. For example, a mother may allow her child to use art materials in an area that does not lend itself to "making a mess" and then become angry when the child does make a mess. All of us have been guilty at one time or another of saying yes to our children when we really wanted to say no. We must try to be aware of this pitfall as much as possible. We are giving our children double messages: the feeling of freedom disappears and the child becomes confused. We must try to be consistent in our behavior. Children become uncertain of what is expected of them if we are continually changing the rules. We talked about Lynne's use of the canvas board. If her mother had blamed her for the destroyed painting Lynne might have felt very guilty about the incident, when in fact she had done nothing wrong. Something similar could be true of Evan, who wanted to build the castle.

Children will draw realistically when they are ready to, and not before. The ability to make realistic pictures usually does not occur before about age 4. Children, like professional artists, often take "artistic license" and draw objects the way they *feel* about them. The first-grade student teacher, who valued the picture of the tree with the purple trunk and brown leaves, was reprimanded by her supervisor for not "correcting" the child. We cannot assume that the supervisor was deliberately trying to stifle free expression, only that she was unaware of its importance.

When I commended my former patient, the junior high school teacher, for his teaching methods, he also told me how difficult it had been for him to maintain his approach to teaching art. The history and music teachers were displeased that the art teacher did not require the students to make workbook covers for assignments from their classes. He held his ground, but it took him a year, with support from the children and parents (like the one I met), to be accepted by his fellow teachers.

I must repeat that I recognize all teachers do not have such rigid viewpoints about teaching art. However, it was judgments like these that inhibited many of us when we were in school. Adult patients, when first asked to draw, frequently tell me they feel uncomfortable because they could never please the teacher in kindergarten or first grade. One man said that the teacher never hung up his drawings because he did not draw like the other children, and he felt that he had "flunked" kindergarten art. I never cease to be distressed when I hear that a child's drawing has not been included in a wall display. This is not just a rejection of the child's *drawing;* it is a rejection of the *child.*

ATTENDING TO DANGER SIGNALS

Whether you are the parent or teacher, you should first recognize the normal indicators of intellectual and emotional growth in a child's imagery. These can tell you whether the child is thinking, learning, and feeling in the same way as normal children around that age.

Children will begin to scribble at around age 18 months to 2½ years, letting us know that they are now able to grasp objects in their hands and move them around to create lines on paper (figure 16).

The scribble takes form and shapes are outlined and placed within other shapes by around 2½ to 4 years of age. During this period of growth, children will begin to draw more complex images and they will experiment with paint and clay if these materials are offered (figure 18).

Artistic skills develop dramatically between the ages of around 4 to 7 years. Drawings become more detailed and more realistic. Graphic images progress from telling a simple story about one object at a time to combining several objects in one picture, telling a more elaborate story.

Differentiation of male and female, completion of figures, ground lines, more realistic colors, and the influence of culture and environment should be evident by the end of this stage/sequence and before the child can move on to the next level of development (figures 19–21).

The child's knowledge of the world expands around the ages of 7 to 11 years. New facts and fantasies about objects in the surroundings are depicted more realistically in art productions, regardless of media. Subject matter may be influenced by interactions with family peers, exciting movies, television shows, and books (figures 22–24).

Danger signals in children's artwork appear in many different forms. For example, if a drawing appears to have been made by a 4-year-old child and we know that child is 7, we should be concerned. Any indication of functioning intellectually or emotionally at an age younger than the chronological age of the child should be viewed as a warning signal (figure 2).

Shaky lines may indicate a learning problem or anxiety. When these are seen in a number of drawings by the same child, it is time to call for help (figure 2).

A form repeated over and over suggests that the child is preoccupied with whatever that form symbolizes (figure 3). This kind of repetition warns us to gather more information.

We should be aware that a child is under some stress if objects in the same drawing are glaringly different in age levels (figure 4). The same would be true if we saw consecutive drawings in the same medium, produced by the same child, that reflected different age levels (figures 33, 34).

The presence of floating objects, produced at a time when that child should be aware of ground lines and should be able to tell a story in pictures, alerts us to the need for further evaluation of that child (figures 1, 5).

Images that are consistently slanted are warning signals

that the child could have a learning disability resulting from a perceptual problem (figures 6, 7).

A child's spontaneous illustration of a particularly violent or tragic event should warn us (figure 8). It is important to explore why the child feels the need to illustrate such extraordinary subject matter.

Finally, we should question both the intellectual and emotional development of any child past the age of 4 who cannot stay within the boundaries of the paper or within boundaries created on the paper (figure 2).

Now that you are able to identify some of the warning signals, how do you use this knowledge? As I constantly remind students, normal physical development is fundamental to normal intellectual and emotional growth. The possibility of physical problems must be considered because they too will interfere with learning. Assessing physical well-being is the first step in dealing with any problem. Pediatricians and family physicians may be your best guide in this.

Let us assume that your daughter is in first grade. Based on report cards and written comments by the teacher, you are pleased to know that your child is doing well in her venture into grade school. Shortly after the second term begins, you receive a call from the teacher asking you to meet with her. Bonnie's mother received such a call, and a meeting was arranged. The young, sensitive and caring teacher was very troubled about this child. Although Bonnie was doing well in her schoolwork, the teacher noticed that she spent considerable time gazing into space and seemed inattentive. The teacher thought this indicated some distress, reflecting a lack of attention from her parents. The teacher knew that there were two younger siblings at home. Bonnie's father, a physician, immediately arranged for a physical examination. The medical report showed that Bonnie had a 60 percent hearing loss in one ear, apparently due to the development of excess tissue after a tonsillectomy performed a year earlier. Medical treatment corrected the hearing loss in a few months, and the gazing into space and inattentiveness stopped.

Where it has been determined that the child has no physical impairments, parents and teachers must find the right people to evaluate the problem and make recommendations. We can illustrate some points about the kind of therapist to choose by analyzing the different danger signals and identifying the professionals most qualified to evaluate the suspected problem, other than an art psychotherapist. Earlier we demonstrated how the art psychotherapist can pinpoint specific areas of concern that would require more discriminating test procedures.

Suppose we feel certain that a child is drawing on a level lower than the chronological age. A psychologist trained in testing methods could determine whether this child's level of intelligence is compatible with the chronological age. A clinical psychologist or a psychiatrist might be consulted to assess the behavior and might recommend additional psychological testing to determine whether there are certain emotional disorders.

This same process could be followed for children whose images float in space, show violent content, or are inconsistent within one picture or from one drawing to the next. These danger signals suggest that the child is very likely to be manifesting some emotional stress or disorder. Intellectual functioning should be evaluated to be sure that the child is not mentally retarded to any degree that would impede normal creative expression.

A child who continually draws slanted images or ignores page or line boundaries or repeats the same line or shape in all artistic creations or cannot draw a line that is sure and direct should be tested for a perceptual problem and a possible learning disorder. Some psychologists specialize in these areas and are professionally qualified to detect such problems.

In chapter 2 we discussed Bobby, who repeatedly drew the image of a "gaping mouth" to master his real trauma of a cleft lip and palate. Often there are similar situations in which a repeated image and lack of attention to boundaries does not mean the child has a learning disorder. The art psychotherapist and psychologist trained in testing measures can confirm that the child is normal developmentally, and may recommend further examination of the child's behavior by a psychiatrist or clinical psychologist.

When we have information that defines the problem, we are faced with seeking help to provide some form of intervention or treatment. The question now is, *Where* do we find professional help and *how* do we judge whether those professionals are qualified to handle the problem?

WHERE TO FIND A QUALIFIED THERAPIST

You can call local colleges or universities and inquire whether they have programs in art therapy, psychology, or social work. If they do, they will undoubtedly have clinics that provide evaluation services. Hospitals and medical schools may provide similar facilities. School districts generally employ school psychologists and counselors and may be able to provide the necessary evaluation.

It is your responsibility as a parent or a caretaker to check the credentials of someone who is going to guide you in helping your child. It is also your right.

The educational requirements of an *art psychotherapist,* as well as the way in which training programs are monitored, were described in chapter 1. The accrediting body for a *psychologist* is the American Psychological Association. This association accredits programs training psychologists. Licensing requirements for psychologists vary from state to state. Most states require rigorous training and supervision in both clinical and testing proficiency, in addition to a doctoral degree—a Psy.D. or a Ph.D. In some states a psychologist with a master's degree can become licensed and thus be eligible for third-party payments.

A *psychiatrist* is a graduate physician (medical doctor or doctor of osteopathy) who has completed at least three years of specialty training in psychiatry after completing medical school. A *psychoanalyst* must first be a psychiatrist and then complete additional training and undergo psychoanalysis with a "training analyst." Psychiatrists become certified under the jurisdiction of the American Board of Psychiatry and Neurology. A psychiatrist, who is a physician, can prescribe medication, whereas a psychologist cannot. There are several national professional associations including psychiatrists and psychoanalysts; these are listed in the Appendix.

A *school counselor* may have a background in social work, psychology, or a related field of study. In this field also, state requirements for qualifications, certification, or licensing are not consistent.

Choosing a clinic to provide the help you seek presents other issues that must be clarified. You should question staff composition—will the child be evaluated by a qualified graduate staff person or an intern? It is often acceptable to have an intern perform an evaluation, so long as the intern is supervised closely by a recognized professional. What is the philosophy and orientation of the director of the clinic? Is treatment based on drug therapy that alleviates symptoms, psychotherapy that focuses on the source of the problem, or a combined approach that is open and sensitive to the needs of the patients? An advantage to obtaining help from a clinic affiliated with a hospital or medical school is that more and more these institutions favor a team approach in which professionals from several different specialties are involved in diagnosis and treatment. This can be extremely effective, especially if the problem involves an organic impairment such as minimal brain dysfunction and an emotional disorder that is functional.

Usually an evaluation is followed by intervention or treatment. The person or persons who perform the evaluations will designate which professional(s) will direct and/ or carry out the recommended procedure. A special school may be recommended for the child who is mentally retarded or has a learning disability. Therapists suggested may include psychologists, psychiatrists, or art, dance/ movement, music, family, or group therapists.

It is your prerogative to question *why* a particular form of treatment is used and *why* a particular therapist is consulted. The credentials of a therapist should be reviewed in the same manner in which you pursued that information in selecting someone to evaluate your child.

Information about the availability of assessment and treatment facilities in your community can also be obtained from a state or county department of health. Each state has an agency that provides both physiological and psychological evaluation of children.

A federal law, Public Law 94-142, the Education for All Handicapped Children Act of 1975, includes provisions designed:

> (1) to assure that all handicapped children have available to them a free appropriate public education;
> (2) to assure that the rights of handicapped children and their parents are protected;
> (3) to assist States and localities to provide for the education of handicapped children; and
> (4) to assess and assure the effectiveness of efforts to educate such children.

If your child requires special tutoring, intervention, or treatment, this law requires that county and state public education systems provide the recommended tutors and/ or therapists at no cost to the family. A copy of this law can be obtained from your state board of education.

To insure competent diagnosis and treatment for your child, you should try to avoid the advice of well-meaning but untrained friends and relatives. Explore the available resources in your community, and if necessary, write to the appropriate state or national office for further information. Be sure to check credentials beyond education alone; experience in treating other children with the same problem as your child's is critical. An individual may have impeccable qualifications, but little or no experience in handling certain problems.

HOW AND WHERE TO FIND HELP

The list of facilities, professionals, and organizations in the Appendix at the back of the book has been prepared to guide you in seeking help when you see a warning signal in your child's creative expressions. Your options may be determined by the availability of qualified people in your community.

Many of the associations publish journals that contain case histories of children with particular problems; these journals are available in many libraries. For the reader who wishes to learn more about these subjects, the Bibliography also includes the titles of books about the creative arts in therapy and about developmental psychology. Parents and teachers must be cautioned, however, not to apply this information without professional guidance.

Books that suggest art activities may be found in hobby and toy shops and libraries. It is recommended that you avoid books in which the projects described limit and inhibit free creative expression for the normal child. Craft kits and coloring books are examples of restrictive art activities. Creative ventures for the emotionally disturbed or learning-disabled child should be guided by a qualified art therapist or other specialists in this area of mental health and education.

Chapter 4

Babble-Scribble Stage/Sequence: Around 18 Months to 2½ Years

In the preceding chapters we presented information, posed questions, and gave some answers about what you can learn from children's drawings. Chapters 4 through 7 provide an in-depth discussion of developmental indicators that can be expressed through children's artistic productions. To help you make a pleasurable journey through the developmental stages of childhood, we have created twins, Adam and Lisa. These imaginary siblings, who represent typical normal children, will be followed through all levels of development from infancy to age 11. A glimpse at their behavior during these periods of growth will help you understand how children interact with people and objects in their environment and how the proper responses from important adults can stimulate learning. Our continued goal is to demonstrate how you can recognize these signs of normal growth in creative work produced by children.

THE FIRST 18 MONTHS

Adam and Lisa enter the world without any complications, and their parents are glad to know that there are no physical abnormalities. All the necessary parts are in place and their first cries are strong. Soon after birth the twins discover their mouths and the pleasure derived from putting something into them. Food is preferred; but as the months go by wonderful substitutes are discovered—pacifiers, blankets, sleeves of clothing, soft toys, an offered finger from an adult. In these early months the twins learn by instinct. Certain discomforts, later to become known as "hungry" and "wet," are announced by loud cries for attention. Gradually the babies learn that this discomfort fades when they are touched, caressed, or fed, or when their soiled diapers are changed. This early intelligence is acquired on a sensory level.

Initially the twins are not aware that comforting feelings come from something separate from themselves. Gradually, they come to know that a certain noise signals that relief is on the way. Most likely this noise is the sound of Mommy's or Daddy's footsteps when they enter the babies' room. Around 6 months of age the twins begin to be aware that some things they feel, touch, and hear are not part of themselves. This is known as the beginning of ego development. The ego is not something we can clearly see or feel, but most of us acknowledge that the "ego" is "self" and that the ego is shaped and formed through these interactions with the environment.

At about 4 to 6 months, Adam and Lisa learn to turn over and sit up; they may try to pull themselves to their feet by holding on to the bars of the crib or playpen. Boys often achieve these accomplishments a little earlier than girls, but having Adam to copy probably inspires Lisa to develop a little faster. In the past, boys were encouraged to be more active physically, and not too many years ago it was believed that the active baby girl would grow up to be a "tomboy"—not exactly acceptable for a girl. Fortunately, this view is changing among enlightened parents, and Lisa is encouraged to test her arms and legs as much as Adam.

Children, however, are not all born alike. Some are more active than others naturally; some are more content to lie quietly and participate in their surroundings by seeing and listening. Adam wants to sit quietly at times, and his parents have learned to match and respond to his movements. This security makes Adam trustful and willing to venture into his small but enlarging world. As Adam and Lisa begin to explore spaces around them, they are reassured that someone is there if needed.

At around 8 months, Adam and Lisa are very upset when they are with strangers. This reaction is typical for this age and is usually outgrown by about 14 to 16 months.

The twins begin to walk at around 1 year of age, moving their arms and legs more purposefully. They know when to hold on to objects to steady themselves, and the growing strength of their grasp gives them confidence. They discover that a familiar face can disappear and reappear and that a ball can roll behind a couch and not be lost forever. In fact, the twins' expanded mobility now makes it possible for them to follow that ball and make it known that they need help to retrieve it. They can also follow Mommy and Daddy into the kitchen, bathroom, and bedroom.

Now that they can grasp more tightly, Adam and Lisa find that feeding themselves is an event. At first they learn by trial and error. They can push the plate, smear the food with the spoon, and actually make something they do not like disappear by dropping it or throwing it. They also learn that playing with food does not make Mommy or Daddy smile. The twins are discovering new accomplishments and creating new tasks to master. This ongoing process is fundamental to learning.

18 MONTHS TO 2½ YEARS

Adam, age 18 months, is sitting in the sandbox. He picks up a toy, examines it, and discards it for another. He pushes the sand around and watches it fall through his fingers. Occasionally he glances at his twin sister, Lisa, but he is much more interested in his own activity. Lisa puts some sand in her mouth and realizes that it does not taste very good, but this causes another problem—the sand is sticking to her wet fingers and she does not like this feeling. She tries to remove the sand from her fingers by rubbing her hands together; when that is not successful, she uses her shirt as if it were a towel to clean off the sand. Giving up the struggle, she reaches for a toy. Her brother's play attracts her attention, and she moves swiftly, trying to snatch the bucket he is holding. Adam is very angry and swings the bucket at Lisa. Fortunately, Mommy has been supervising closely. She moves Lisa to another place in the sandbox and gives her another bucket.

Adam and Lisa are behaving like most 18-month-old children. Their attention span is short, and the children are distracted easily. They are not yet ready to share toys or play together, and they are unable to communicate with words. Adam may know a few words, but not enough to tell Lisa what he thinks about her reaching for his toy. He can make his feelings known with body movements, and he can call an adult to rescue him. Both Lisa and Adam will babble to themselves and to others; their acquisition of language will depend largely on how much they are encouraged to learn words.

Around this same age the twins are becoming aware that they can resist certain expectations from the adults who care for them. The word *no* has been mastered and is used so often that this period and the next six months to a year are often referred to as the "negative stage"; parents have called it the "terrible twos." This is a necessary stage—the child is testing limits in an effort to define acceptable behavior and establish independence.

Around age 2, the twins will gradually be faced with either submitting to toilet training or displeasing the adults they have come to trust. Toilet training is a normal battle for control and is an important time for Adam and Lisa to learn how far they can go before Mommy and Daddy say no. Lisa may become toilet trained a little earlier than Adam, but this is not unusual. While the development of sphincter control is generally equal in boys and girls, boys usually are slower in complying. Both children will have "accidents" for months and maybe years to come, but that is to be expected.

The twins will delight in being given crayons and paper; if they sit close to each other, they will draw on each other's paper. At first they will not be able to stay within the edges of the paper and will make marks on any available surface. They must be watched to make sure they do not put the crayons in their mouths. By the time the twins are 2, they should be enjoying making lines in all directions, interspersing them with dots. The children will recognize colors and eventually learn to say the names of these colors, with the help of Mommy and Daddy. With prodding they will name their scribbles, although they probably do not have a particular object in mind when they start to draw.

The following are several examples from the twins' real-life counterparts.

Holly's mother is an artist, and crayons and paper are always available. Holly, at 2, spontaneously produced many pictures of scribbles.

While Holly's scribbling traveled all over her paper, Hal, also 2, preferred to draw separate pictures in different sections of the paper (figure 37). Hal has just been introduced to paints and, with close supervision, handles them remarkably well for his age.

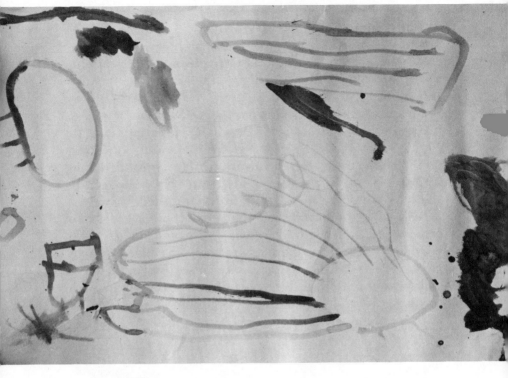

Figure 37

At 2 years 10 months, Joey is able to use a crayon in different ways—rapidly and loosely to fill in the area at the top of a sheet of paper, and more tightly and slowly to create the form at the bottom (figure 38). When his mother asked him to describe the picture, he said it was "a steam shovel with a man inside."

The way small children progress in handling various art materials tells us how well they are developing fine motor control—the ability to progress from drawing loose random lines with crayons to drawing fine controlled lines with pencils or felt-tipped pens. Some children will develop this fine motor control faster than others.

Because it is believed that children do not have a plan in mind when they begin to scribble, we would not expect to be able to detect any danger signals in scribbled images. However, there should be some cause for concern if a child was not interested in "playing" on paper with crayon by age 2. This kind of situation could reflect other developmental delays and should be investigated.

Figure 38

A steamshovel
with a man
inside.

Chapter 5

Word-Shape
Stage/Sequence:
Around 2½
to 4 Years

Adam, 3, is sitting on the floor in his bedroom, playing with miniature cars. With one in each hand, he zooms them around the space in front of him, crashing them into each other at one moment and whizzing them past each other the next. He makes loud noises to accompany the cars' movements and intersperses these sounds with commands to the imaginary drivers. Lisa, his twin sister, is in her bedroom playing with her dollhouse. She is busily rearranging the furniture and telling an imaginary Mommy doll to "hurry and make lunch; the children are hungry."

Around 3, all children start to be interested in specific toys and "play out" activities, imitating parents or other caretakers, stories they have heard, or television programs they have seen. Mimicking special adults in their lives pleases Adam and Lisa greatly. It also helps them to handle uncomfortable feelings that result from disagreements with Mommy and Daddy.

The twins will often play side by side, but not yet *with* each other. Sharing toys is still difficult and may need mediating—Adam and Lisa do not want to share *any* of their possessions. This proprietary attitude extends to their beds, special plates, and eating utensils. Certain blankets and bedtime companions, such as a teddy bear or doll, become important objects in their world. In the normal transition period, in which children are giving up some of their attachment to their mother, father, or other early caretakers, these personal claims are necessary substitutes to help them in this natural process of becoming separate from these adults.

During the word-shape stage/sequence, words are repeated for pleasure at first. Gradually they are connected and take on more meaning. Adam and Lisa speak in monologues to themselves. Even when stimulated by a question or command from another child or an adult, the response still sounds like a monologue, unrelated to the question or command. At this age words are clear, but complete sentences are more the exception than the rule. Adam and Lisa will learn more about words and sentences by example from their parents and other adults, but they will still continue their monologues for a while. They cannot be expected to hold conversations before they are ready. These skills will be accomplished individually.

By age 3 the twins are aware of themselves as separate persons and will assert themselves frequently to confirm their place in the household. Only in the previous few months have they felt very comfortable playing in a room by themselves; they still leave their play frequently to make sure that a special adult is nearby. Mealtimes are less messy, but the struggle over toilet training has not been resolved. By definite words and actions, Adam and Lisa demonstrate that they will decide to regulate their bowel and bladder habits when they are ready. Their preoccupation with this process is often reflected in their going out of their way to avoid unpleasant odors. This will probably stop when they are more willing to comply with adult requests.

Adam and Lisa delight in walking, running, and handling new objects, but their movements are not always smooth. The twins run around the house excitedly, sometimes bumping into furniture and breaking things. Like other 3- to 4-year-old children, they do not always want to admit they are responsible for the damage. They will blame another child or create an imaginary friend or animal to be the target for Mommy's or Daddy's anger. When they grow to understand that someone can be angry with them but still love them, the necessity to blame imaginary friends dwindles. However, imaginary friends may still be invented to serve as playmates until the child goes to school.

Early in this stage/sequence, scribbling is still evident in the twins' drawings; gradually certain shapes will emerge and forms will be outlined. The children will begin to organize forms on paper and will show an early sense of balance by drawing both large and small shapes. Some of these forms will be combined to look like recognizable objects, although the shape may be primitive and somewhat abstract. The world in which children live will influence the objects crudely symbolized in their drawings and clay sculptures. They particularly enjoy rolling clay into long strips and round patties and drawing shapes they will tell you are monsters. Adam may master the scribble more quickly than does Lisa, but within the year, like most children their age, their skills will be similar.

Here are some more examples from real-life counterparts at this age.

At 2½ Nicole's mother was showing her how to use paint. Together, they created a picture Nicole titled "Crickets." Paint was a new experience for this child at this age. Nicole's mother told us Nicole was delighted with the "smeary" quality but needed help to keep the paint on the paper.

Hal was just past 3 when he did this drawing with colored felt-tipped pens (figure 39). Hal's parents furnished him with a rich array of art supplies and he spent much time experimenting with them. In this picture he scribbled, drew forms inside other forms, and added some lines. He stayed within the boundaries of the paper very well, considering the many images he wanted to create.

Figure 39

It was a pleasure to meet Tony, who attended a nursery school where I was known as the "art lady." Tony was one of the most self-sufficient 3-year-old children I had ever met. Like Hal, he spent most of his free time drawing or painting. During my four weeks at the school, Tony invited me to look at his drawings or draw with him whenever I was free. The children worked on easels, and it was not easy to control dripping paint. Tony discovered that he could make interesting designs from these "accidents" and began to create them consciously. This is a remarkable accomplishment for a 3-year-old child. Tony's rapid advancement in artistic development was demonstrated in two other situations.

One morning Tony asked me to sit with him while he drew with colored chalk on a small chalkboard. He wanted to produce a tree, grass, and sun, and asked me to help him with these images. I took another chalkboard and in a simplistic way illustrated these objects and suggested that Tony try to copy them on his chalkboard. I was not surprised that he was able to do this successfully. I was surprised a week later, however, when he greeted me with a detailed chalk drawing of these same objects. He was delighted that he had been able to replicate a picture that had been erased the previous week.

Tony's capacity to recall the instruction he had received and to reproduce the objects so well over a period of eight days reinforced my impression that he was a very bright child who functioned on a more advanced level than did most 3-year-old children. His imitating my drawing suggested that he was also beginning to seek out adults he wanted to imitate. This behavior usually occurs closer to 4 or 5 years of age. The nursery school staff reported that Tony was advanced in all areas of cognitive and emotional development, supporting my perceptions of his creative expressions.

Figure 40

Holly, at 3, has combined shapes and lines to produce "a man with funny hair" (figure 40). The familiar scribble and her description of the picture focus attention on the top of the head; emphasis on the head is typical for children of this age. Developmental psychologists believe that the rapid physical growth experienced by all children between birth and 4 or 5 years creates a feeling of imbalance in the child. Efforts to master this feeling, probably first expressed by drawing large and small shapes, are now reflected by placing unrealistically large objects on the top of the head, by making one limb larger than the other, or by exaggerating the size of hands and feet. Holly's awareness of the opposite sex is also emerging—a natural course of events for children this age. There are two important men in her life, her father and her older brother, so it is no surprise that she calls this figure a "man."

WARNING SIGNALS AT 3

The most significant warning signal at this age is contin-
uous scribbling with no evidence that the child is able to
outline shapes within the scribbles or produce spontaneous combinations of shapes and lines. It is important
to note whether the child is advancing from babbling to
saying words and incomplete sentences. These two developmental progressions generally occur at about the
same time, and the strong presence or absence of advancing language or drawing skills should cause concern.

In chapter 2 we introduced Indira, the little girl from
India who created the same images in paint as her Western
playmates. "Doing art" with me at her nursery school,
Indira was very intrigued with colors and typically used
them in a way that pleased her but had little to do with the
actual color of an object. On one day in particular, she was
using a variety of colored markers to draw forms that she
named (figure 41). Indira called the large yellow shape a
"horse," the turquoise form a "cat," and the orange figure
an "umbrella." Between these images she drew some scribbles but told me they were "nothing." Finally she picked up
a pencil and drew a very light form in the lower left

Figure 41

corner. She said this was "Mr. Uppity." This child's choice of pencil to draw a human form was as surprising as her name for this barely visible figure. She had made this image distinctly separate from the others—it had no color and was a human instead of an animal or inanimate object. She would not tell me anything about "Mr. Uppity," and I would not press her to discuss it. It was obvious, however, that it symbolized something or someone that did not deserve the colorful attention she gave the other images.

My experience in assessing children's drawings led me to explore Indira's behavior with the nursery school staff. I asked whether she handled situations that distressed her by withdrawing. The teachers said that when Indira was asked to do something she did not want to do, was having difficulty with another child, or was overly tired, she could not express her feelings, although she had a good command of English. She would either remove herself physically from the situation or have a temper tantrum so a member of the staff would be compelled to take her aside. We discussed the possibility that "Mr. Uppity" symbolized Indira's feelings of separateness in an environment where she was a minority. We also discussed the fact that she was the youngest of five children and perhaps was treated in an infantile way at home, making it more difficult for her to handle the usual demands of nursery school. We all agreed that more communication between Indira's family and the nursery school staff was critical in helping this 3½-year-old girl make the transition from home to school less likely to result in episodes that forced her to find infantile ways to remove herself.

As Adam and Lisa move into the fourth year of their lives, they will be faced with new experiences that will help them grow and learn new skills. These experiences and the new challenges they bring will be discussed in the next chapter.

Chapter 6

Sentence–Picture Stage/Sequence: Around 4 to 7 Years

4 YEARS

Adam, 4, sits on the living room floor, playing with the lifelike doll he had requested and received the previous Christmas. He is "Mommy," spanking his baby brother for "not drinking his bottle." Meanwhile, Adam's twin sister, Lisa, is busy in an upstairs bedroom. Preening before a full-length mirror in her mother's out-of-style clothes, she relays instructions to an imaginary baby-sitter. The beaded dress droops in folds around Lisa's ankles and trails on the floor; a large, floppy hat nearly covers her small, round face, completely hiding half of her head and all of her hair.

Four-year-old Lisa, like most children her age, is preoccupied with her own interests. She imitates her mother and other important women in her life, pretending to cook and clean if her mother is a homemaker, playing dentist if her mother is a dentist, and "dressing up" like her mother. Hair styles, makeup, and clothes are fun if they are also important to the mother or a mother figure.

More than likely, Lisa has mastered her urine and bowel control and is quite pleased with herself. Mommy and

Daddy are pleased, too. Naturally, there are times when Lisa does not like her interactions with Mommy. For example, if Mommy is too busy caring for the new baby brother to give Lisa the amount of attention Lisa wants, it might not be such fun to dress up and *care* for dolls. Lisa might be more likely to spank the doll or throw the "bad" doll into a corner.

Whether or not children are able to act out their feelings, they may want to put some of these feelings into their drawings and may even demand that their mother display them on the family showcase—the refrigerator door. This can also happen in the nursery school or day-care center where the teacher or aide represents a mother figure. The 4-year-old girl will have fun imitating the teacher, too, and sometimes be displeased with the teacher because of real or imagined slights. It takes some time to conquer the feelings that accompany being separated for a long stretch of the day from the mother at home. Lisa may express her thoughts and feelings about this new experience in destructive play—or in her drawings.

Adam, like most boys his age, is still strongly attached to Mommy. He will be 5 or 6 before he begins to imitate Daddy. Now, however, it is not unusual for Adam to imitate Mommy in the same ways Lisa does; playing with dolls, doing housework, or playing dentist. Adam's feelings of jealousy about his baby brother will be similar to Lisa's. Adam, too, may resent being taken to a day-care center or left with a baby-sitter. We said before that boys are slower in learning to control urine and bowel movements, and Adam may still be struggling with this developmental task.

Like Lisa, Adam will express feelings through play and drawings. He and Lisa will learn that destructive play results in punishment. Learning this is important, because during this period in their young lives Adam and Lisa begin to *understand* right and wrong. They learn what is acceptable social behavior, what makes those large, powerful adults around them angry and what makes them smile. At the same time, Adam and Lisa realize that drawing or painting their feelings and thoughts remains an acceptable and rewarding activity. They know these "creations" are not always *understood* by those same large and powerful adults, but these adults are always *pleased* with the children's artwork. The more Adam and Lisa learn to behave like Mommy, Daddy, and Teacher, the more they will tell us in their drawings how they feel about these limits and expectations.

During this stage of their growth Adam and Lisa develop a greater awareness of objects around them. They now can produce recognizable images, even when such images—a bed, for example—are out of sight. At first they will draw only one object on a sheet of paper. Gradually, Adam and Lisa will begin to draw several objects on the same page. These objects may have no realistic relationship to each other. The door on Adam's house will be too small for the person he has drawn on the same page. The flower in Lisa's drawing will be larger than the person she draws on the same page.

Depending on the kind of stimulation they receive at home and at school, this is the age at which Adam and Lisa may begin to read words and learn to converse socially. Speech continues to be for the most part a monologue, but it is now interspersed with attempts to be understood by others. Intellectual skills naturally improve with age, making the twins' verbal responses to others more appropriate. They understand and can offer criticism, commands, requests, and threats. As the social need to communicate verbally increases, Lisa and Adam will learn more ways to speak with others.

The following drawings were produced by real-life children the same age as Lisa and Adam.

We met Scott briefly in chapter 2 (figure 19). Let us look

a little more closely at this image produced when Scott was 4. The scribbles and shapes within shapes are joined to represent a figure. One big circle is the head and two little circles inside are just where the eyes belong. A line marks the mouth. Scott knew that there are arms, legs, hands, and feet, and connected them to the head. It looks as though he was trying to scribble hair but did not quite connect it to the top of the head. It does not matter that the hair does not quite connect or that there is no torso and nose. What *does* matter is that Scott was beginning to put together the artistic skills he had mastered over the previous 2½ years, to make something that even adults can recognize as a human figure. This drawing represents a classical developmental image that psychologists call a "tadpole" figure.

Dayna, also 4, was still mastering the word-shape stage, drawing shapes within shapes and beginning to connect them to represent a figure, all within the same picture (figure 14). Dayna was still drawing some of the *images* that gave her pleasure in the not-too-distant past. The embracing of these images is much the same as Linus's need (in the "Peanuts" cartoon) to carry a security blanket everywhere he goes. However, emerging from these early images is a figure that now includes a head similar to the one in Scott's drawing (figure 19). Dayna's drawing of the head includes a nose; she has made another circle for the torso and added arms and legs.

Dayna, the third child in her family, has two older sisters and a baby brother. Both parents have careers outside the home; Dayna's mother is an artist who encourages her children to express themselves freely with a variety of art materials, and the children have no known developmental problems. An older sibling is naturally a model to copy, and a new baby in the house, who receives much attention, arouses the wish to be a baby again. These normal mixed emotions are expressed in the blending of the stages and sequences and the transition from one period of growth to another within one drawing. Later you will see other creative drawings from Dayna and some from her sisters.

Keith, 4, enjoyed attending nursery school. He was not interested in learning to read, much preferring to have someone read to him from his older brother's books. Keith did love to draw, however, and was provided with an abundance of drawing materials by his parents, teacher, and artist grandmother. For an art activity at nursery school, Keith was asked to depict "Spring" (figure 42). He had no problem pasting bits of colored paper to represent the foliage of a tree and drew lines down under the colorful collage to create the trunk. The image is bright and cheerful, reflecting Keith's bright and cheerful feeling about spring and the art activity. It is no surprise that the colors he chose are not realistic. Children of this age often select colors they like and pay little attention to the actual color of an object.

Figure 42

Figure 43

At age 4 years 7 months, Keith was able to draw a picture with more than one object (figure 43). On the same piece of paper he drew a house, a tree, a sun, clouds, and rain. Typically at this age, houses can be taller than trees; sun and rain can be present at the same time. Keith tells us that he now sees and knows these objects and elements in his surroundings and is able to represent them in a recognizable way.

Houses, suns, and trees appear frequently in children's drawings. The houses often represent security and warmth. Suns and trees represent powerful objects in the environment. A tree may also represent self. In Keith's drawing these three objects symbolized the three most important objects in his young life—his mother, his father, and himself.

Lilly, 4 years 2 months, painted a family portrait—mother, father, and child (figure 44). Lilly's father is a colleague of mine, and Lilly drew many pictures that were used as examples in art therapy classes. Although Lilly has an older sister, the sister does not appear in this painting. Lilly was just learning to deal with her mother and father as two separate people but was not ready to include her older sister in any family portrait. She solved her problem in a wonderful way, simply by omitting her sister from the painting—a natural solution at Lilly's age.

Figure 44

Around the same time, Lilly used crayons to draw a house, a sun, and a lamp on a table. In that picture, Lilly substituted a lamp for the symbolic tree. Like other normal 4-year-old children, Lilly is telling us symbolically which objects are important in her life at this time. Lilly drew the lamp on the table outside the house on the same page. She drew a face on the sun. Interiors and exteriors painted side by side and faces drawn on suns are *not* unusual images at 4. These two examples of Lilly's creativity illustrate her ability to handle crayon and paint and to represent objects graphically somewhat better than most children her age. This could be attributed to the fact that, in addition to her natural talent, drawing and painting are encouraged and rewarded. Lilly knows that her artwork is often presented to *college* students who are learning to be art therapists.

Hal at 4 has discovered King Kong (figure 45). He combined his mastery of the scribble, lines, and shapes to create an image of this monstrous gorilla towering over many other forms, some more recognizable than others. Hal was trying to tell a story and make some order out of his impressions of someone else's fantasy—one that could be frightening to any child of 4. We do not know that Hal was frightened, but we do know that he wanted to show us some of his thoughts and feelings about King Kong. Hal's artistic and cognitive skills are not far enough advanced at this age to make the story very clear. However, his control of the art materials and his efforts to communicate so many details in one picture are more likely to occur at 5 years of age than at 4. We said before that Hal was encouraged at a very early age to experiment with different art materials, and his innate abilities have helped him to learn more quickly than most children.

Ray, 4, who lives across the country from Hal, also was impressed with King Kong and drew the monster hovering over a "boat, fish, and lobster." Like Hal, Ray was also

Figure 45

trying to tell a story about this gigantic creature, much bigger than all the other objects in the drawing: Ray did not yet connect forms in a logical, coherent fashion, but this is not expected at age 4.

We have mentioned that children around 4 years of age are naturally learning to deal with their mother and father, and that many of their pictures around this time include three objects—usually parents and child or house, tree, and sun. Ray's representation of this important threesome includes his father and two other members of the family "in the woods." He used the familiar scribble appropriately to fill in the bodies, hair, and ground. Ray's mastery of shapes within shapes led to the creation of eyes and mouths. We believe he expressed personal feelings and thoughts about two of the figures by placing them so close to each other and separate from the third figure. If we had asked, he might have told us why he did that—but this really was not necessary. Ray has invested much energy and time in creating a colorful picture; when he was finished, he was eager to move on to some other activity.

The drawings by Hal and Ray of King Kong and Ray's picture of the three family members (excluding himself) are examples of how children begin to express on paper strong impressions from the world around them. In the process, they master the feelings and thoughts stimulated by these people and events.

WARNING SIGNALS AT 4

I met Leon when he was 4 years 1 month old. He was a delightful, stocky boy, who was very articulate for his age and played nicely with the other children in the nursery school. It was surprising, therefore, to see his drawings. Most of the time he produced line drawings more typical of a 2- or 3-year-old child than of a 4-year-old. One day he outlined a shape, extended lines from it, and told me it was "a kind of hamster" (figure 46). I was struck by the fact that he seemed *aware* that it was not an adequate image of a hamster. Why was there this inconsistency between his behavior (which appeared normal for his age) and his artistic development (which reflected a lower level of intellectual and emotional development)? I learned that Leon had been hospitalized several times during the previous year for serious ear problems. Illness and hospitalizations that interrupt the normal developmental process can cause what psychologists call "developmental lags." Leon was *not* showing signs of regression—going back to a previous level of development. Rather, he was telling us he was still a little behind the other children in some areas of maturity.

Figure 46

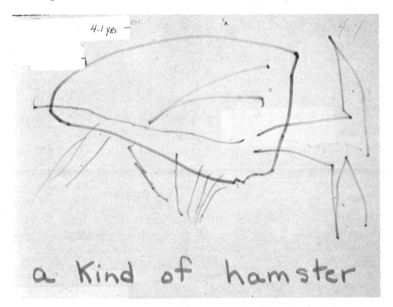

Figure 47

In chapters 1 and 2 we discussed Bobby, who was drawing "gaping mouths" on all the faces of figures. Aside from
this one unusual repeated image, his images were varied
and similar to those of other children his age. One of those
forms (figure 47), unnamed, is very similar to Leon's "kind
of hamster." This picture was made by Bobby when he was
3 years 4 months old—almost a year younger than Leon
was when he produced figure 46. This drawing is normal
for children Bobby's age, but comparing these two drawings will help you understand what we mean when we say
Leon is creating images on an earlier developmental level.
Almost a year younger than Leon, Bobby is easily drawing
a form that is still difficult for Leon.

A lag in development is not unusual for a child who has experienced repeated hospitalizations within a year. This development was not observable in play, but certainly would have been apparent when Leon started school. He was showing us through his art that he needed more support and encouragement than his peers in order to help him make up for lost time.

The painting that Harry, 4, made in nursery school I refer to as a "muddy blob." I watched Harry paint, and he simply kept applying one color on top of another, smearing it all together, like a 2- or 3-year-old child who just discovered paint. A few weeks later I noticed that Harry was drawing circles with a pencil and trying to fill them in with orange paint. In the first picture, Harry *was* regressing—returning to an earlier level of development. We know that because the second picture tells us that Harry is very capable of drawing circles with a pencil and controlling paint. These two very different images within a period of several weeks are a signal to explore Harry's world further. How does he behave? Is there anything about his home environment that might explain this erratic creative expression? In Harry's case we were able to learn some answers.

Like his drawings, Harry's behavior in school and at home also was erratic. Sometimes he would act like an extremely mature 4-year-old; at other times he would whine, cling to his mother (at home) or the nursery school teacher, and reject the attentions of anyone else. The director of the institution in which this particular nursery school was housed shed some light on Harry's problems. This little boy's mother was expecting another child in a few months. Mother and father were a bright, intelligent, and sophisticated couple. They lovingly believed that sharing the process of the pregnancy would help Harry accept the new baby more easily. Sharing meant inviting Harry to touch and see his mother's growing body and giving him information about the birth process.

Harry's parents meant well in trying to share the details of his sibling's birth, but this kind of information is *too much* for any 4-year-old to handle. Harry's drawings and behavior told us he vacillated between the need to regress by smearing paint and clinging to home and school "Mommies" and the need to try to control his anxieties by drawing circles to contain paint or by acting like an adult. Many of us believe that if we are "open" with our children and tell them "everything they need to know," they will grow up without fear of sexuality and attain mature sexual behavior. I believe this is true—but we must also be *aware* of and *sensitive* to the fact that children will ask questions, especially about birth and sex, *when* they are ready. Giving too much information too soon, and inviting a 4-year-old boy to touch his mother's growing abdomen and breasts at a time when he is naturally struggling to be like his father, can only cause confusion and anxiety. At this age all little boys are still emotionally attached to their mothers (more will be said about this later), and this kind of intimacy can only create havoc, which Harry was manifesting in many ways.

In chapter 2 we discussed Michael's difficulty with learning because he had a perceptual problem (figures 31 and 32). We knew that Michael, 4 years 10 months, was showing signs of emotional problems as well, and a picture of his family told us a little about some of his sad and angry feelings and how he was coping with them. This drawing was produced several days after Michael's evaluation. By this time he was very comfortable working with me and was more than willing to draw his family. At the bottom of the picture he drew what appeared to be a fence, and added the first figure, which he described as himself "shooting and killing robots with my ray gun." The second figure was his brother, Tom, who was not shooting because "the robot was his best friend." He identified the third figure as his father who was "not seeing" and "not shooting." When asked, Michael said that his mother was not in the picture because "she would get hurt."

Michael's parents had been separated for a year, and his picture probably represents some of the loss Michael felt about his father's absence from the home. Although there had been no contact between them for a year, Michael wanted his father in the picture. As in a dream, Michael has reversed events. *He* could not see his father, so he drew him as someone who was present but "not seeing." Children this age cannot understand the concepts of divorce or separation on an adult level. Michael felt he must explain the loss to himself in some way. Like other children in such a situation, Michael was angry. Some children turn this anger on themselves and decide they are responsible for a parent's "leaving"; some children blame the remaining parent. I suspect that Michael was very angry with his mother and may even have fantasized killing her—feelings and thoughts that he had learned must be suppressed. The drawing is Michael's creation. *He* is the only person doing the shooting and *he* has decided to leave his mother out of the scene so she would not get hurt. In Michael's cast of characters, *he* is the only one who could hurt her.

Michael's drawings and behavior give us an idea of the extent of his difficulties in trying to create order in a disordered household. This effort was made even more difficult for him because of his perceptual problem. As we studied his drawings more closely, we gained some direction to help us plan intervention and treatment for Michael and his family.

5 YEARS

Around age 5, Adam and Lisa begin to respond differently to Mommy and Daddy. They also have become more aware of the differences between girls and boys.

Lisa still wants Mommy's and Teacher's attention, but now seeks more attention from Daddy—the same kind of attention she sees him giving to Mommy. The pervasive intrusion of television has speeded up the awareness of male-female interactions for Lisa and her twin brother. Lisa is beginning to "flirt" with Daddy and other adult male family friends and relatives.

Adam, on the other hand, not only wants Mommy's attention, but wants to treat her the way he sees Daddy treat her. Traditionally, this would have meant wanting to climb into bed with her and imitating his father by assserting himself around the house. But times are changing for the 5-year-old Adams of the world. They still want to be physically close to Mommy, but the familiar male "macho" image is not necessarily the norm. Adam may enjoy sharing the quiche with both Mommy and Daddy and playing catch with Mommy.

Play activities with other children provide an opportunity for 5-year-olds to act out some of their fantasies about adult relationships, and it is around now that Adam and Lisa will play "house" or pretend to be a doctor, salesperson, or carpenter with each other and with other children. An interest in "war games" becomes evident; whereas in the past this scenario was strictly for the boys, Lisa and her girl friends now will participate frequently.

Images of people are drawn a little more realistically at age 5, and telling a story in a picture is evidence of better organization of thoughts. This is aided by the natural advancement of intellectual and artistic skills. These normal accomplishments will appear when Adam and Lisa have mastered all the artistic skills they have learned up to now, and this may occur at different times for them and some of their real-life counterparts.

The following drawings were created by 5-year-old boys and girls. You have already seen drawings done by some of these children at an earlier age; it is interesting to follow their developmental paths through their drawings.

Figure 48

At 5 Keith attended Sunday school regularly, describing to his parents what he was learning about the creation of the Earth. To reinforce their lessons, Keith and his classmates were asked to draw the seven days of creation. To illustrate day six, Keith drew the creation of Eve from Adam's rib (figure 48). Adam is definitely bigger than Eve; his hair goes up; Eve's hair goes down. We have also seen some of Keith's artwork at age 4 (figures 42 and 43).

Male-female differences become more explicit at age 5. Even though Keith has omitted hands, feet, and facial features, he has communicated his growing awareness of the differences between his mother and father by drawing Adam, with short hair, larger than Eve, with long hair—just like his mother and father.

Keith had learned that on the seventh day "God rested," and with the typical 5-year-old's ability to understand this and represent it, he drew a figure sleeping in bed. Keith *knew* that bed was a proper place for resting.

At home Keith often turned to ever-available art media. One day he learned that trying to make a tree with paint was not as easy as he thought it would be—paint was messier than crayon. Keith persevered, however, and created a recognizable tree with surprisingly realistic colors. At 5, the bottom of the paper is a logical baseline, and the way Keith "spread" his tree over almost all of the paper told us he did not feel inhibited about expressing himself artistically. This is also true of Keith's verbal communications.

Nicole, also 5, is the daughter of an art therapist mother and a photographer father. She always has free access to all kinds of art materials. Nicole had just acquired her first bicycle, for which her father had bought a bell and streamers. She and her father went bike riding together, and she drew a picture to commemorate this exciting event (figure 49). At age 5, little girls want to be with their fathers, and Nicole was no exception. She appears complete, at the top of the picture, but much smaller than her father on his bicycle. Nicole's mother has unusually long legs, and it probably is not a coincidence that Nicole and her father both have unusually long legs in the drawing. She was still combining characteristics of both parents in her drawings.

Figures in profile are not usually seen in the artwork of 5-year-old children, but the open invitation to draw in Nicole's home and her exposure to photography had made her more expressive than most children her age. It had also made her aware that she could recall and *record* a special time.

Previously we discussed Scott's progressing awareness of the differences between girls and boys and his ability at age 5 to put more than one object in the same picture. At the same age, Scott drew a boy, a girl, and rainbows. Scott at 5 wanted to be his mother's little boy as much as he wanted to be like his father, so the figures represent the important people in his life as well as himself. There is now a new baby sister in the family. We do not know whether the girl in this picture is supposed to represent Scott's mother or his baby sister, but *she* is easily identified as female. The two figures are the same size, and Scott was telling us some important thoughts he was having at that time. If he has drawn the girl to represent his mother, she is now *small* like Scott; if the girl is a representation of his new sister,

Figure 49

she is now *big* like him and does not need his mother's undivided attention. While we know Scott naturally wanted to be close to his mother, he drew the boy leaning away from the girl, but looking at her; at the *same* time he showed her looking away from him. Scott was beginning to realize that it was time to move away from his mother.

Scott, like most children, was fascinated with rainbows. He had learned about them from stories, and there are three rainbows in his picture. We said previously that three related objects in drawings are one of the ways a child symbolizes a mother/father/child relationship, and Scott's rainbows may be a way of keeping his threesome separate from the foursome that now makes up his family.

Children learn about clowns from stories and perhaps from television or a trip to the circus. Scott drew a "clown and a boy bouncing balls together" (figure 50). The figure of the clown is complete; the figure of the boy is not. Clowns are awesome—they do all kinds of amazing tricks that make children laugh and cry and even feel scared. Around this age fathers can also be awesome, especially when little boys are trying to be like them. Scott told us in this drawing that the little boy (Scott) could "bounce balls" with the clown but that he was not as complete as the clown (the father).

Scott's rainbow drawing and clown drawing were personal expressions of his efforts to master moving away from his mother and identifying with his father.

At this same age Scott drew a picture that illustrated how children will create images that are a sign of past and present sequences of artistic development. Scott wanted to draw a turkey, which is not an easy bird to represent on paper. His effort was a return to combining shapes within shapes and scribbling to fill in the turkey's body. It is common for a child to try to draw something before he or she has acquired the skills to produce it, especially if, like Scott, he is interested in everything around him.

Figure 50

We discussed Dayna's drawing at age 4 (figure 14). Becca, Dayna's next older sister, was 5 when she drew a smiling little girl apparently skipping through the flowers (figure 51). The large head on the figure and the omission of arms are not unusual at this age. Human beings experi-

Figure 51

ence a greater amount of physical growth between birth and 5 to 6 years of age than during any other five-year span of life. This enormous growth spurt stimulates a natural striving for physical balance that is likely to be reflected in children's drawings around this time. Up to around age 7, it is *normal* to see figures drawn with one leg or arm larger than the other, heads bigger than bodies, big hats and bows on tops of heads, and even the omission of some parts of the body. This would be *abnormal* if we had other evidence that the child was well past this stage/sequence and capable of drawing people and objects with realistic proportions.

The next three drawings discussed are good examples of images produced by normal 5-year-old children, and show different manifestations of a striving for physical balance.

Tom's drawing was given to us by his teacher; we know nothing about him other than his age. In his wonderful picture Tom clearly distinguished male from female, but drew an oversized head on one figure and unequal arms and legs on both figures; he used the same lines for hands and feet. It is very interesting to us that he makes the female larger, but gives the male a more "aggressive" image. This probably reflects the *normal* process of this period—Tom is beginning to identify with the important male figure in his life and become less dependent on his mother.

Cleo, 5, presented us with a delightful example of "balancing" her female form and probably some of her thoughts and feelings about being like the special adult female in her life. A hat with an extended ornament sits atop the oversized head. Arms hang down almost to the ankles, and legs are longer than the upper portions of the torso. There is no sign of the lower torso. Colors are used unrealistically, and Cleo skillfully combined familiar shapes within shapes, scribbles, and lines. Her "lady" reaches from the top to the bottom of the paper. It is apparent that Cleo was having no problems expressing herself—at least artistically.

Some children will move into the storytelling sequence sooner than others. Martin, 5, was telling us about a character who is sitting on top of a large form and brandishing weapons (figure 52). The two rectangular scribbled forms to the left of his head are not part of his story— they were inserted to cover his real name, which was printed very well for his age. Martin has put what looks like a hat on the head, has made one arm larger than the other, and has even made the weapons consistent with the size of the arms. The legs are almost hidden, but Martin was showing us his wish and natural need to begin to assert himself.

Figure 52

WARNING SIGNALS AT 5

We have already presented some examples of warning signals at age 4; these examples will overlap and may be seen in the drawings of children aged 4, 5, and 6 years, depending on the child's individual rate of progression and problems. The following are additional examples of warning signals that may be seen at ages 4, 5, and 6.

Kim's floating house was presented in chapter 1 (figure 1). At 5½ years of age, Kim drew a house similar to the houses drawn by other children of that age. However, children of that age do not usually draw houses floating in air. If not yet able to draw a ground line, a child will use the bottom of the page as a baseline. Regardless of the country or climate in which they live, children learn from storybooks that houses often have chimneys and will show this in their drawings. Frequently there is even smoke coming from the chimney. Also by 5½, children are normally interested in representing people, making some early distinctions between female and male. Intellectually they are able to put more than one object in a picture.

Kim's drawing has none of these normal indicators. A professional art therapist's view of the images in Kim's drawing raises questions about his home life. Who cares for him? What are his relationships with these caretakers? Why does the picture make the therapist feel that Kim is lonely, isolated, and depressed? And, finally, how does the drawing reflect Kim's behavior in nursery school?

This is what was learned. Kim was in a European orphanage until the age of 3, when he was adopted by a couple from another country and brought to a land that was new to him. Both countries, incidentally, experience all four seasons, and houses heated by fireplaces are more the rule than the exception. When Kim showed signs of difficulty in adjusting to his new environment, his adoptive parents had him psychologically tested, and I met him while he was attending nursery school.

Kim could not play with the other children and rarely paid attention to group activities, although his command of the new language was more than adequate. He saw a psychotherapist once a week, and a volunteer aide in the nursery school was assigned to stay with him constantly. It was believed that, based on his history, he needed one person to relate to and trust before he could form relationships with other staff and children.

One experience typifies Kim's abnormal behavior. I had been at the school every day for several weeks, and while Kim kept his usual distance from me, I was not a "stranger"; he knew me by name. Kim was playing alone in the sandbox when I approached quietly and asked if I could watch him play. He became very excited and told me I had to turn my back and stay that way until he was finished—I could *not* see what he was making until he gave me permission. I did as he requested, turning around only when he said it was okay. I admired the form Kim had created from the sand and asked him to tell me something about it. He acknowledged my praise but would not talk to me and would not look me in the eye. All of this behavior is abnormal for a boy of this age.

I learned that Kim was *not* encouraged to draw at school, either alone or with the other children. His therapist told me that his mother frequently *made* him draw at home and was often critical of his drawings; the teachers wanted to avoid this same kind of stress. I wanted to see what Kim would express through his drawings. While playing house with him in the kitchen the aide handed Kim some paper and felt-tipped pens. Silently he chose green, and the image of the little house emerged.

What we suspected when we looked at the drawing was supported by Kim's history, behavior, and psychological testing. He was a bright child, but seriously emotionally disturbed. Intellectually he could represent the parts of the house and put them together correctly, but the floating image, the emptiness of the house, and the space all around it told us that in many ways Kim still felt like a "floating abandoned object." Fortunately, Kim's new parents knew the value of seeking help for him and for themselves in order to help this little boy grow emotionally.

6 YEARS

Around age 6, the separation of the sexes becomes more pronounced for Adam and Lisa. Children begin to act out male/female roles, and normally they imitate and gradually begin to identify with the parent of the same sex. While there may still be some merging of Mommy and Daddy in pictures drawn by the twins, the female figure has become more *female* and the male figure has become more *male*.

More and more, Adam and Lisa are becoming aware of what those large, powerful adults who direct their lives deem to be right and wrong. The twins will try to avoid or control behaviors that result in the wrath of these adult godlike persons. The impulses, feelings, and thoughts that stimulated and inspired these now unacceptable acts have not gone. Although children are not always aware of these feelings consciously, they still can feel the need to express them. And feelings *do* get expressed in fantasy, in play, and in drawings—all acceptable outlets for children's emotions.

For Adam and Lisa, adjusting to first grade is a new, exciting, and demanding experience. Kindergarten helped in the transition from home to school, but now they must spend at least six hours away from home—twice the time they were away last year. However, Adam and Lisa are developing their intellect and sharpening their learning skills. They are beginning to read and write short, complete sentences. This provides them with additional ways to express their emotions. The twins are learning to solve problems by dealing with Mommy and Daddy together and individually and by learning to relate to a new teacher for a longer period of the day. They need these skills to adapt to that new environment in their young lives called school.

Adam, Lisa, and their real-life counterparts draw objects more realistically, begin to use color more appropriately, and tell pictorial stories in greater detail.

Brent, at 6, was much more aware of the differences between boys and girls than Scott was at 5, and this is to be expected. These two drawings (for Scott's, see figure 50; for Brent's, see figure 53) illustrate how, within a year, normal development progresses so that drawings express greater details, more recognizable images, and compliance with parental rules.

Brent's immediate world has consisted of four people (not three) for some time, and he showed us that he has accepted that fact. This was consistent with his good adjustment to school. Although Brent did not put a ground line in his family picture, the feet of all figures are planted firmly on the bottom of the page.

Brent is the older brother of Keith, whose drawings at 4 and 5 were shown previously (figures 42, 43, and 48). Unlike Lilly at age 4 (figure 44), Brent acknowledged his brother's presence in the family and included Keith in the picture, along with his mother, his father, and himself.

From the time he was very young, Brent was interested in using any materials he could find to express and display his creativity. His family portrait was produced with colored pencils and pieces of tapestry he found in his mother's sewing basket. He cut out a skirt for his mother and pants for his father, Keith, and himself.

Figure 53

In the drawing, Brent was almost but not quite as tall as his father. His mother and father were drawn in a distinctly different way: the father wears a hat and the mother has hair. Brent still used parts of both parents to represent himself. He has a hat like his father's and a nose like his mother's and has drawn in the upper torso of himself and his mother in the same way—with the familiar scribble. Brent did not allow Keith to be as big as his parents or himself, but he did give his little brother *some* recognition. By age 6 Brent has learned that it would not be favorable to exclude 3-year-old Keith or draw him separately from the rest of the family. Brent put a tall hat on Keith so this littlest member of the family could be equal in height and even granted him the father's belly button. However, he did put himself between his mother and Keith, with himself taking a position similar to his father's—next to his mother!

Looking closely at the drawing, we can see that Brent

gave his father enormous hands and each successive family member smaller and smaller hands. We do not know whether this means that Brent views his father as the most powerful family member or whether the large hands on the father, as well as the hats on heads, indicate that Brent was still striving for balance. It may mean both. We know that a certain object (such as a hat or body part) may symbolize more than one thing for the person who draws that object.

Whatever the meaning (and even Brent may not have been consciously aware of the meaning), there is a wonderful aspect to this artistic creation. Brent's feelings and thoughts related to his family were being expressed in a way that tells us this 6-year-old boy was learning rapidly and knew what was expected of him. He was organizing his family relationships in an orderly fashion that was comfortable to him and acceptable to everyone else.

One weekend Scott's family went fishing. When they returned, 6-year-old Scott drew how he felt about the adventure. Scott did not catch a fish, and neither did his mother or little sister. But Scott had discovered that a good way to compensate for disappointment is to draw what he wished would have happened. He could not quite bring himself to draw a boy catching a fish—that might have been too close to telling how he really felt. Instead, he drew a series of pictures of a *girl* catching a fish.

Scott's story begins with a picture of a sunset, water, and a fish; he titled it "Jumping Fish." The colors were appropriate; the sun set on the horizon line where water meets sky; and the fish really appears to be jumping. The next drawing, titled "Fishing Girl," shows a figure with a big head with eyes, nose, smiling mouth, and lots of hair. The figure stands on the bank and throws a line to a fish in the water. There is also a bright yellow sun in the upper righthand corner. The third drawing has the same figure, this time without hair, standing on the bank and holding

Figure 54

the line with the fish dangling from it (figure 54). On this, Scott wrote "She caught a fish." In the final drawing the figure is smiling, holding the fish on a chain. The line and hook are above the bank, and the figure appears to be falling down the slope of the bank. On this drawing Scott wrote "She hase it on her chane."

When we look back at Scott's ability to draw objects and people at age 5, we might think that his graphic skills have regressed in the past year. This is not true; he has actually improved those skills. In fact, Scott was now able to draw water and sky meeting at the horizon line, a readily recognizable fishing line, a chain, fish, and a riverbank. He was even able to write complete sentences with only a few words misspelled.

What *did* happen between the ages of 5 and 6 was that Scott learned to overcome his disappointment by fantasizing—in this example, by fantasizing that another child had caught the fish. It is not surprising that the other child was called a *girl,* as his baby sister had been on the trip, and like

Brent, Scott was adjusting to including her in his immediate world. In this four-part picture story, Scott expressed his wish that he had caught a fish and did not even pretend to himself that he had been the lucky fisherman. He mastered his disappointment by drawing a girl, who by the fourth picture could easily pass for a boy—like himself.

Jon, just 6, was *still* working on the problems of dealing with the three most important people in his world—his mother, his father, and himself. Jon was also learning about castles and kings and queens; he used these objects to master the usual triangle in a small child's life: two caretaking adults and self. Jon's drawing is a castle complete with turrets on the top, a wall extending from each side, three archways, and two sets of three windows (figure 55). There is one figure in each of the three archways; two figures are equal in size and larger than the third. On the heads of the two larger figures there are objects resembling crowns, whereas the smaller figure appears to be wearing a hat.

Figure 55

We have said before that it is not unusual for children around this age to show different levels of development in intellectual and emotional growth within the same drawing. Jon's portrayal of the castle is done well for a child of 6. His ability to draw figures has developed a little more slowly. Solving the problem of more grown-up relationships with his mother and his father is a major task for a child, and Jon was in no hurry.

Dayna, 6, did not accept all her siblings as readily as did Scott and Brent. We have already met Becca, Dayna's next older sister (figure 51), and we will meet Elysa, the oldest sister, in chapter 7. We know that a brother was born when Dayna was 2 years old.

Using a pen with remarkable skill for a 6-year-old, Dayna drew a balloon with a gondola. In the gondola are *five*, not *six*, people. We assume that one sibling is missing because there are three small and two large figures. The figures are so tiny that it is hard to tell male from female, but the largest person is smiling, standing in a row with three small figures and another larger one. We compare this with Dayna's imagery at 4 (figure 14).

The title on Dayna's picture at 6 is "Something that will make me happy." She has told us that a wonderful fantasy for her is to ride in a balloon with just the people she wants with her. She also demonstrated that she could write almost complete sentences.

Cleo has told us that she, too, has learned a number of new skills in the past year. At 5, she drew one large figure with female characteristics just beginning to appear. In that drawing she also reflected her feeling of imbalance through the natural distortion of some of the limbs and body parts. At 6, Cleo created an idyllic scene of a couple out walking their pets (figure 56). Her images of the woman and man are well proportioned and illustrate some skillful handling of the medium—the woman has a shoulder bag and the man has a bag in his hand. Cleo tried to

Figure 56

show the pet leashes around the wrists of the couple and even drew a house in the distance. Her artistic efforts tell us that she was observing what people do and what the details about her surroundings are. She was aware of trees, birds, butterflies, sky, and ground. As she tried to represent them realistically, Cleo learned more about them. In this process she has naturally developed her learning skills.

We know very little about Cleo, but her couple drawing leads us to believe that she was romanticizing what it would be like to be walking with her own male partner. Like all girls of this age, Cleo may have been learning that to be like her mother means she must also imagine her own male partner. The one she would really like to have belongs to her mother.

Halloween is a time that inspires the creation of wonderful images, which are shown in the following examples from children at different ages.

In preparation for Halloween, Shelley, age 6, drew four people dressed for the occasion. They are all carrying bags, and I imagine they are on their way to visit homes for "trick or treat." The figures are all complete; males are differentiated from females, and the colors could be very appropriate for costumes. The four figures could very easily represent a family. Because family members are the most familiar people to a 6-year-old child, it is very possible that Shelley has used her own family members as models.

Shelley's ability to draw figures, organizing shapes and forms to tell a story, indicates that she has very advanced learning skills. Her illustration of figures touching each other in a natural way makes us believe that touching and holding in a healthy way are usual occurrences in her home environment.

At 5, Tom drew a picture containing both female and male figures; we described how the female figure was the larger of the two. At 6, however, Tom told us that he wanted to stand alone by including only a male figure in his drawing (figure 57). The boy Tom has created looks as if he is flexing his muscles and taking a very assertive position. I suspect that the decision to draw just the image of the boy evolved as Tom was working. He did not center the figure, and had he wanted to include another person there is space on the paper. Tom was beginning to identify with the important male figure in his life and was trying to be less dependent on the important female in his life. His "strong" boy is not grounded by either a line or the bottom of the paper, but Tom has been moving slowly into this new role. When he feels more secure he will probably plant his feet firmly on a baseline.

Figure 57

Keith, at 6, was still trying to master paints. We have already described his success in creating a tree with this difficult medium at age 5. Keith now produced two figures and a building that looks like a castle resting on a green ground. He was progressing well and did not hesitate to experiment; his pride in this image is evident—he wrote his name in bold brush strokes across the top of the page.

WARNING SIGNALS AT 6

In chapter 2 we discussed Bobby and described some of his "gaping mouth" drawings from age 3½ to 8 years (figures 25, 26, and 27). In many of his drawings, Bobby had expressed his feelings about his cleft palate and the surgery he underwent to correct the condition, and at 8 he showed his mastery of this real problem. If we did not know Bobby's history and how normally he had developed, we might have cause for concern when looking at his drawing at age 6. He had combined all the artistic skills he had learned, but all of the figures are floating and unconnected. The repeated jagged lines in the figures and around them and the different levels of development in one drawing all could be warning signals if we were unfamiliar with Bobby's history.

In this case, however, we are very familiar with Bobby and realize that his latest drawing is another creative expression of how this child dealt with his problem. The "gaping mouth" that was repeated over and over in those early drawings is not present here. Instead, the jagged lines of the teeth appear on different parts of the bodies and in lines on the paper. At this age, Bobby probably was feeling much better about himself but may still have been expressing some suppressed anger through his imagery. This drawing is discussed in this section on warning signals only to illustrate how viewing one isolated drawing, without other background information, could lead us to form inaccurate conclusions.

Arthur's graphic representations were discussed first in chapter 2 to illustrate how one art therapist worked with learning-disabled children in a special school setting (figure 30). I refer again to them here because they are very good examples of images a 6-year-old child of average or better intelligence would draw when hampered by a perceptual problem. We have learned that children with this difficulty will "perseverate"—they will repeat the same answer to different questions or become "stuck" on a word or idea, unable to move on to the next task. In drawings we see this in a repeated form or line. Most often it is a line, and in each of Arthur's pictures he draws a series of lines. In figure 30, the lines make a trail of smoke. Arthur's other images show that he has made a great deal of progress in organizing his thoughts. In one drawing, Arthur illustrated what appears to be a tree and a sun. However, the series of lines is still present around the circle that forms an apparent treetop; these lines also radiate around the sun.

We have traveled with Adam and Lisa and their real-life counterparts as they made their way from home to school, formed a normal attachment to their mother, and spread that attachment to include their father. Gradually they established some independence and greater awareness of self. By now this sense of self will begin to be expressed in the way they conduct themselves, particularly around each other and their parents. Adam and Lisa know they are *different* from each other—they have known this for several years. Lisa knows she will "grow up" to be like her mother and Adam knows he will "grow up" to be like his father. There is still much they do not know about male/female differences, but they will ask for more information when they are *ready*. They are learning that the bathroom is a "private" place for one person at a time and that bedrooms have definite ownership. This natural need to identify their own "space" should be encouraged and respected as much as possible.

The next four years are a time for Adam and Lisa to acquire the knowledge and everyday living skills they will need to face adolescence.

Chapter 7

Fact-Fantasy Stage/Sequence: Around 7 to 11 Years

7 YEARS

Adam and Lisa, just arriving home from school, race each other to the refrigerator for a snack. Mother tells them that there are cookies on the table and juice in the re-frigerator—and to be quiet because their baby brother is napping. The twins collect their afternoon treat, and on the way out of the kitchen, Mother hears Adam announce that he is going outside "to play street hockey with some of the guys"; Lisa announces she is on her way upstairs to "check on her Cabbage Patch doll family" and is expecting her girl friend, Anne, to come over soon to see her doll collection.

Around age 7 Adam and Lisa are very likely to go their own ways whenever possible. Both children have identified with the parent of the same sex, and for the next year or so Adam will prefer to play with the boys and Lisa will prefer the company of girls. Some parental values become so much a part of their personality that now they often act and sound like their parents on issues of "right" and "wrong." They are also acquiring new role models—teach-ers, television and movie stars, and sports heroes.

School continues to introduce Adam and Lisa to a variety of new learning experiences. At their own pace they will learn through reasoning how to move from the beginning to the end of a process and back again. Thought processes, in general, are gradually becoming more logical. They know the difference between closed forms, for example, how circles differ from squares, and they can distinguish between curved and straight lines.

The social need to communicate with peers and adults outside the home speeds the development of language skills. The use of words becomes more meaningful—words are now an important aspect in determining the kinds of new relationships that will be formed and how Adam and Lisa will handle encounters with other children and adults. Like most children this age, the twins still talk to themselves, usually when struggling to solve some problem.

By now, Adam and Lisa are not likely to draw any figure that cannot be recognized as male or female. More and more their drawings will include a ground line and horizon line. The consistent appearance of these lines tells us that Adam and Lisa are at the proper stage of development for their age, with their two feet settled firmly on the ground as they learn more about their expanding environment.

At age 7 figures may well be facing front and not showing much movement, but this will gradually change as the twins' world stretches from home to school and they engage in more active play with their new friends.

A child may use a certain color for drawing because it is the only one available or because it is the one that appeals most to the young artist's curiosity and interest in experimenting. Only when important adults press for more realistic images do Adam and Lisa begin to suppress some of their natural spontaneity and creativity. Ideally, Adam and Lisa will be given art materials and no *adult* rules. Left to express themselves freely, they will first draw what they *know* and then what they *see*. As their cognitive and artistic skills improve, children's art expressions will tell us what they *know* and *see* and *feel*.

Let us look at some drawings from real-life 7-year-old children.

Eva, 7, told us much about herself in just two drawings. In the first picture she drew a figure sitting on a horse; the way the horse's legs were drawn gives the impression of movement. Rider and horse are facing what looks like a gate or fence; in horseback-riding terms this could represent a hurdle. The felt-tipped markers were used so heavily that it is not easy to see exactly where ground meets sky, but the horizon line is there. It is also difficult to tell whether the figure is male or female. The proportions of the objects—excluding the oversized sun marked with her name—are relatively the right sizes. Eva, on her horse, could jump over the hurdle.

In the second drawing Eva let everything spill out (figure 58). Obviously, she was familiar with the mythical story of Pandora's box: Eva titled this picture "Pandora and the Box." Pandora, with long black hair and fancy dress, occupies the center of the picture. Around her are symbols of some of the concerns now felt by this 7-year-old child: good and bad, blindness, "cold feeling," germs, death, and poison. Some of these "worries" may seem a little unusual for such a young child, but I believe that television makes even young children aware of these possibilities. Eva also may have heard of some of these "conditions" from her parents—her mother is a special education teacher and her father is a physician. She has also included spiders, fighting, and a good spirit, objects and ideas we would expect her to know.

We do not know what Eva was thinking when she drew these pictures. They were given to us by her mother, who felt that Eva's intensity when drawing the pictures and then putting them aside, meant that they may have had

Figure 58

more meaning for Eva than some of the other artwork she produced. This probably is true. What more marvelous symbol than something like a "hurdle" can a child imagine to tell us what it is like to be in school, away from home most of the day, and required to form new relationships with important adults and peers?

Eva was still sometimes uncertain whether she should *act* like a girl or a boy. But she did know that she *is* a girl, and Pandora (a fantasized representation of herself) looms large and queenly over all the problems that may be connected to the "hurdle" in the first picture.

Brent, whom you met at age 6 (figure 53), was 7 years 5 months old when he created a fantasy world on paper. Brent had discovered science fiction, a typical interest of boys this age in our outer-space-preoccupied society. Instead of blasting off into space, however, Brent went under the water. Drawing on a sheet of lined notebook paper—Brent will draw on anything that has a usable surface—he created an underwater world complete with an Earth transporter and an Earth police station. Like Eva, Brent gave himself a fantasy world, but with built-in controls: the Earth police station had an open door to the "real" world through his Earth transporter.

Children, like adults, also want to escape the "real" world when problems occur and will tell us in their drawings about the natural turmoil they feel as they move through and around home and school. This *movement* is expressed over and over in the images of magical, mythical, and scientific fantasies. For the healthy child, there will always be a growing connection to the "real" world.

Becca, 7, was beginning to make plans about what she would be when she "grew up." Naturally, these plans will change many times before she makes her final choice. Becca did two drawings within a few days of each other; together they tell a story about who she is and what she fantasizes she will be.

In the first picture Becca drew a smiling girl (herself), holding up one hand as if she was waving (figure 59). On a piece of paper that she attached to the drawing, Becca wrote, "When I grow up I will be a doctor." She already knew that it was acceptable for women to consider entering what once was traditionally a male profession. The girl wears a dress; a stethoscope is hanging from her neck. Less than two weeks later, Becca drew a "big" girl holding the hand of a "small" boy. There is something hanging down the front of her dress in this picture, too. Although Becca did not say so, the hanging object resembles the

Figure 59

stethoscope in the earlier drawing. The small boy may represent Becca's younger brother.

At this stage Becca had mixed feelings—this was a time to be like her mother and to be independent of her mother. Becca's drawings tell us how she was thinking she would fulfill both of these needs. She will be a "lady doctor"—*not* like her mother, and a lady who takes care of little children—*like* her mother.

Becca was one year older than her sister Dayna, who was introduced at age 6. By the time *Dayna* was 7, she was not ready to plan for the future; she still wanted to play out-

Figure 60

side with the dog and drew her wishes in a colorful image of a little girl and a rather large dog (figure 60). Not yet comfortable with thinking as far ahead as Becca did, Dayna nevertheless made concessions to growing up and being female. She put rouge on her cheeks and elaborate eyelashes on her eyes. As we have mentioned before, the oversized head is seen often in the drawings of children this age. In addition to aiding in the effort to achieve balance, this overemphasis on the head also may indicate a need to pay more attention to the new experiences at school.

We shared with you the drawings Keith did in nursery school when he was 4 (figures 42 and 43), his images of the creation of the world when he was 5 (figure 48), and his painting of a tree when he was 5. At 7, Keith combined paint, pencil, and crayon to create a cartoonlike image of a snowman. At the same time he did a crayon drawing of a smiling boy with very broad shoulders who is tossing a football (figure 61).

We have said before that graphic images reflect some part of the artist that produced them. In these two pieces of artwork, Keith was telling us different feelings about himself. In the picture of the snowman, he was saying that sometimes he felt like a huge blob and a stupid fellow—the snowman *is* saying, "Boy! I'm a stupid feller." It is also interesting that Keith had drawn three small houses. There is a tree between the two on the left, and the third house is alone near the edge of the right side of the paper. At the time he drew this, Keith's family consisted of his

Figure 61

older brother, father, and mother. We also know that very often people draw the same number of objects in a picture as the number of people in their immediate family. We think that in this picture the houses represent the three males in Keith's family (including himself), and the tree represents his mother. This combination of objects and symbolic representations is not unusual for a child this age. Keith, like many 7-year-old children, is still working through his relationship with his mother and father. We also think that Keith's "stupid feller" snowman probably reflects his normal feelings of being inferior to his older brother. He was also aware that he was small for his age.

In his next drawing (figure 61), Keith strongly compensated for any feelings of inadequacy by making himself a football player and writing his name in large letters on the picture (he did not sign the drawing of the snowman). Keith's father played fullback for his college football team, and Keith's brother, Brent, plays Little League baseball.

We will see more of Keith's and Brent's drawings as they move toward adolescence.

The next seven drawings and paintings to be discussed were given to us by a teacher in a public school, and aside from their names and ages, we know nothing about these children or their families. They are all in second grade and adjusting well to school, according to their teachers. We are very pleased to include these art expressions, because they are all different and wonderful examples of what individual children tell us when they are 7.

Shirley wanted us to know that she knows what looks male and what looks female. She drew all of the body parts for each figure and used color in a creative yet realistic way. Shirley knew that sky is different from ground but was still not aware that in a drawing the sky and ground meet at the horizon line.

Deana drew three whimsical figures riding what looks like a dinosaur. The three important people in her life (parents and self) are transformed into a fantasy. One of the figures is carrying a smaller figure—we do not know whether this represents a sibling, but it may. Deana's colors are not completely realistic, but that only helps to tell us that she is a creative and imaginative child.

Putting herself on paper as a "big" person can help a child feel like one. Rae has used almost the entire space of the paper to create this image of a woman in a hat and high-heeled shoes (figure 62). Rae seemed to know about horizon lines; the blue sky meets the green ground.

Figure 62

George almost ran out of paper trying to create his "big" man—he did not have enough paper for the arms. George handled the paint very well; he artistically used a light color for the man against a dark background.

Dick learned to draw objects like wheels on bicycles and to make fancy numbers. In his drawing he still used the familiar scribble and shapes within shapes to create a sky, but soon he will reach the developmental level of his peers and learn how to draw sky, ground, and a horizon line. He did know how to represent himself. He drew a smiling boy with hands on hips, standing beside a very original creation of a bike.

Elly's beautiful painting illustrates her continued interest in important objects in her environment—house, tree, and sun (figure 63). She also included a bicycle, flowers, and a winding path leading to the house. The colors are realistic: a tree is green and brown, a house could be yellow and red, and a bicycle could be red. Often the way children draw windows and doors on houses make them resemble faces. The sizes of the objects in this picture are not quite in proportion to each other. The organization of the picture, especially the way Elly has placed the house sitting on the horizon line, indicates that, if asked, she could produce all that is absent in her image without any difficulty. But why ask her to do that? Elly took "artistic license" and painted how she *felt* in and about her surroundings. She felt balanced and secure in this colorful place.

Betty, like Keith and Elly, was still mastering that special group of three. In her own individual expression she created three ballet dancers. The shorter hair on the figure in the middle makes us think this is a male figure, but only Betty could tell us that. Her dancers are on their toes on a red stage and look as though they are *moving*. Betty probably liked the color blue and decided to give her group blue mouths to match their blue eyes. It is her picture, so

Figure 63

she should decide what it will contain. Betty's smiling, moving figures, in ballet costumes and toe shoes, tell us that this little girl, at 7, was learning about new people and new activities and was having fun. Her picture made us smile, too.

WARNING SIGNALS AT 7

A very *important* aspect of warning signals is that they sometimes tell us to wait. As at a yellow light in a traffic signal, we must *stop, look,* and *wait,* before taking any steps toward intervention or treatment.

In chapter 6, we described Bobby's "gaping mouth" drawing as an image that, if studied without knowing more about Bobby, would cause concern. Because it is as important to know when *not* to do something as it is to know when to *do* something, let us discuss two more examples of Bobby's drawings at age 7.

At 7, Bobby created a Father's Day card for his "Douddy." At first glance this picture might appear to have been produced by a younger child. However, the way in which Bobby used different seals to design the card, and his lettering, tell us that Bobby's ability to organize his interests and thinking is normal for his age.

Bobby's second picture, obviously drawn for the same occasion, includes a picture of himself and "Daddy" (figure 64). Bobby was still drawing figures floating in space and still mastering shapes within shapes, but his figures are much more complete, telling us that he has made tremendous developmental progress in his self-image and artistic skills over the past year. Bobby was catching up with his peers, and there was thus *no* cause for concern.

Figure 64

Figure 65

There is considerable cause for concern, however, when we look at the picture of a house drawn by Rafe at age 7 (figure 65). You saw one of Rafe's drawings in chapter 2 (figure 29). In this new picture he drew a house floating in space and told us he could not make straight lines—he had to draw over some of the lines to make them meet. He did know what elements make up a house; like Kim (figure 1), Rafe has drawn windows and a door. He has even included a chimney. But the struggle he portrayed in trying to draw a house is a warning signal of a problem that requires further investigation. Rafe, as we discussed in chapter 2, was a child of average intelligence who had a learning disability. This drawing alone would be a warning signal— a signal reinforced by his other drawings.

8 TO 9 YEARS

Adam and Lisa, now 8, continue to go their separate ways. Adam prefers to spend his time with peers of the same sex. At school he will seek the company of other boys during lunch and free periods; after school he will also spend his time in outdoor activities or indoor games with these same boys whenever possible. Competition in school achievement and in sports becomes evident, and Adam chooses friends whose accomplishments in these areas are similar to his. Adam and his friends sometimes talk about the girls in their classes and may even tease them occasionally. Usually at this age, however, they keep their distance.

Lisa's friends are girls she has met in school or in her neighborhood. Like Adam, she much prefers to be with peers of the same sex during and after school. She frequently invites girls over after school to do homework or play with dolls. Lisa and her friends also compete with each other, but this competition is more likely to be associated with scholastic achievement than with sports. Lisa will probably become friends with girls who have similar interests; this is normal. The girls are beginning to notice the boys, whisper and giggle about them, and decide together who is "cute" and who is a "creep." However, they keep their distance from the boys.

This year and the next two are interesting years for the twins. As they learn new things in school, meet new classmates and teachers, and become acquainted with the parents of their friends, they realize that not every child or every adult is the same. It is surprising to them that a "friend" they thought liked the same things they did has suddenly moved on to other interests and other peer groups, and sometimes they feel left out. It is also surprising to them that some parents are more strict or less strict than their own. The twins sometimes think that they have the *greatest* parents, while at other times they are certain their parents are the *worst*. This usually happens when there is a conflict about being allowed to go somewhere or acquire some new toy or piece of clothing. It is not unusual that during this year and the next the twins may fantasize that they are adopted and even dare to ask their parents for "proof" of their birth.

Adam and Lisa become much more aware of these differences among parents or caretakers during this year and the next two years. They also begin to realize that some of their friends lag *behind* them in some areas and that some seem to be leaving *them* behind.

By ages 8 and 9, children's drawings become more and more realistic and reflect school pressures to improve their verbal, writing, and reading skills. Some children still work on art projects at home, but for others the pressure to excel academically closes the door to appreciation of the arts and free expression. Children who continue to express themselves through art will express more movement and fantasy, at the same time showing more realistic proportions in the relationships among objects in a drawing.

We now describe some drawings from real-life 8- to 9-year-old children.

Dayna, 8, was asked to write and illustrate a story for school. In her story she described her return from school and the things she did when she arrived home. To depict this daily event, she produced a drawing of her house, with the large circular path leading to it, trees, and other familiar details. This drawing is of special interest to us because it showed how Dayna had incorporated her ability to make shapes within shapes, resulting in realistic images that tell a story. This project was directed by the teacher rather than being a spontaneous expression; you saw Dayna's more expressive images produced when she was 7 (figure 60).

Elysa, Dayna's oldest sister, drew a self-portrait at 8½ years. She showed a profile of a little girl standing in the grass, seeming very content, with a big smile on her face. This picture told us that Elysa at 8½ was still drawing a figure with a large head and had not yet learned how to represent the horizon line. But her skill in drawing a profile and attention to detail also told us that she was expanding her artistic skills—at her own pace.

We said previously that Halloween is often a time that inspires young artists to create fantastic images. Brent, 8 years 7 months, struggled to put all of his images on one piece of paper and discovered that he was running out of space (figure 66). A baby-sitter was in the house when Brent was working on this picture, and Brent expressed his frustration to her. She suggested that he tape another piece of paper to the bottom of the first. Brent was delighted with this solution—he had learned how to solve a problem of space on paper. He now had enough room to include all the objects that for him represented Halloween—a haunted house, flying witches and bats, pumpkin faces, and a black cat hunched on a fence. We met Brent's family earlier in a picture he created at 6 (figure 53) and learned of his underwater world at 7.

A friend had a wonderful way of teaching the children in her classroom new words to add to their vocabulary. She would give the children a large sheet of paper and instruct them to write eight new words on this sheet and do a drawing to illustrate each word. She would also have them *move* to the words and make a *sound* they thought would be connected to each word.

Figure 66

Ron, 8, did this series of images to show his understanding of "run," "shoot," "kick," "jump," "fight," "work," "cry," and "bark" (figure 67). Looking at his individual representations, we can see that Ron understood the words and had learned how to draw movement and action, finding his own symbols for different words and ideas.

Nina, another child in the same school class, was given the names of states and countries—Texas, Mississippi, Washington, New York, Mexico, California, Iran, and Hawaii and asked to draw them. At 8, Nina was learning a great deal about different places and had her own personal objects to represent each place symbolically. For example, she drew a river for Mississippi, a tall monument for Washington, and palm trees for Hawaii. To her, each object had a special meaning for that city or country. The way that Nina made connections and solved problems presented to her told us that she was progressing very well in school and was becoming more aware of the world around her.

Etta, 8, still focused on three objects and showed us that on some level she was still preoccupied with the most important relationships in her young life—her mother, her father, and herself. Etta painted a colorful picture of three figures. From the clothing on the figures it was difficult to tell whether they are females or males; in real life both boys and girls wear pants. However, two of the figures have long hair, suggesting that the one with short hair may be a male figure. Etta was able to portray movement—the arms are all in different positions. She also made the sky meet the ground at a horizon line and could control paint to produce a complex image.

Figure 67

Figure 68

Sonny, 8, was experimenting with different media and discovering how to create intricate designs in two colors (black and white), using stems and flowers as his inspiration (figure 68). The control of the lines and the organization in this picture tell us that Sonny has noticed his surroundings and could organize his impressions of them.

WARNING SIGNALS AT 8 TO 9

In previous chapters we met Scott, a very creative child who has received a great deal of encouragement to draw at home. At 8, Scott produced a very organized drawing by placing one color next to another to make different shapes (figure 69). But most of his previous drawings showed a freedom with the medium and subject matter that was not present here. Even when Scott mastered his dislike of a snowman and drew him as a robot at age 7½, he was more expressive and creative. Because I know Scott and have been very familiar with his artistic productions since he was 3, I wondered what stimulated this very tight, structured drawing. In fact, it reminded me very much of the kinds of drawings produced by nurses and medical students when asked to draw for the first time in years (this observation was discussed in chapter 3). I asked Scott's mother if she had any idea what may have stimulated Scott to produce this image, so unlike any of his others.

His mother did have an answer. Scott's father had gone out of town on a business trip for a few days. Shortly after he left, Scott received a call from a friend who told him he had just learned that *his* father had gone away and was never returning. Immediately after reporting this tele-

Figure 69

phone conversation to his mother, Scott went to his room, did this drawing, and then moved on to another activity. It was also very unlike Scott not to show his (artist) mother his pictures and discuss them with her. Scott's mother and I both believe that after his friend's news, Scott probably began to worry that maybe *his* father would not return either. The concentration required to make these colored shapes within shapes (a preoccupation with an earlier form of expression) seemed to relieve some of the anxiety we believe Scott was feeling temporarily—an anxiety seen in the pressured way Scott used the crayons.

Learning to make designs with new media in school is expected at ages 8 and 9, as we saw in Etta's painting. However, when a child produces a spontaneous picture that is so very different from everything else she or he is creating at that time, as Scott did, it is important to notice whether this kind of expression continues and to try to learn if there is anything troubling the child. In this case the anxiety was based on a fear that, for Scott, was not a reality. Scott did not duplicate this image, and there was no need to discuss this picture with him.

Becca, at 7 years, drew a picture of herself with a stethoscope around her neck (figure 59) and wrote about her wish to be a doctor when she grew up. We predicted that she would change her mind many times before reaching a final decision. At 8, Becca drew a picture of a figure she titled "self-portrait" and attached a story in which she reported that she washed dishes and wanted to be an artist. We would expect Becca to want to identify with her mother (her mother is an artist) and would also expect to see this drawing indicate normal developmental progress in the same way her earlier ones did. At 8, Becca's drawing of a figure was less mature than her drawing at 7. Like Scott, Becca seemed to be telling us that something was troubling her at that time. Being aware that a sudden shift in creative expression *may* be a warning signal will alert us to observe our children's developmental progress more closely.

Figure 70

We did not know what was going on with Becca at that time, but I was able to share this observation with Becca's mother so that she would be sensitive to Becca's struggle with identity issues during adolescence. The last we heard, Becca has grown up just fine; she is in college and doing very well.

At around 7 years, Elizabeth had some feelings of anxiety related to her school performance. Her concerned parents discussed this matter with her teachers; a medical examination revealed no obvious physical reason for the anxiety. Elizabeth is a beautiful, bright, talented little girl, who loves to draw. For this reason it was recommended that she meet with me to try to determine why she was so worried. At the time of this writing, Elizabeth and I continue to meet, and she agreed to share two of her drawings because we both know how much they tell us.

During one of our first meetings, shortly before she was 8, I asked Elizabeth to draw her family (figure 70). From the beginning, I was impressed with her intelligence and artistic talent. In the picture she made a good effort to draw her father, mother, and older brother very realistically and in proportion to each other, but Elizabeth drew herself as a Cabbage Patch doll rather than as a *real* person.

Some months later, Elizabeth drew a picture of what she did when she was angry or upset—she cried (figure 71). Here, the image of herself was drawn much more realistically as the real, pretty young girl that she was. Elizabeth, her family, and I knew that these two drawings, made months apart, showed us that Elizabeth was beginning to have a better image of herself and was more able to express her feelings than she could in the past. She still drew members of her beloved Cabbage Patch doll family, but they were no longer self-portraits. Her images of family members also improved.

Carl, 8, was in the same school class as Ron (figure 67) and Nina, but his drawing tells us that he was not doing as well as they were. Some of the illustrations for his words look as if they were drawn by a much younger child. The way he drew the faces and hats for "Mexico" and the moving arms in his figure symbol for "New Jersey" showed us he was probably of average or above-average intelligence. However, the fact that he did not complete figures and that he drew in a constricted, colorless way at this age warns us that he may not have had a very good self-image. Normal children this age usually feel pretty good about themselves, and those *good* feelings about self would be needed to help Carl face the normal upheaval of adolescence. Carl may have been having some emotional problems. Fortunately, his teacher was aware of this and knew where and how to obtain help if necessary.

Figure 71

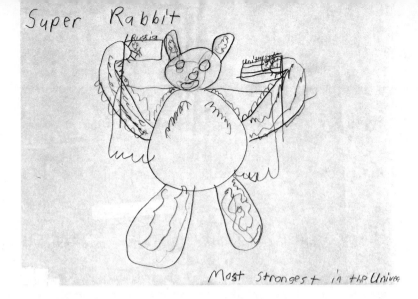

Super Rabbit

Rusia

United States

Most Strongest in the Univer

Figure 72

Ken produced three drawings during the school year when he was around 8. He was a learning-disabled child who attended a special school. Ken's problem was that he is hyperactive; his drawings show us he had difficulty staying within boundaries, real or imagined. His picture of the "Battle of Gettysburgh" indicated he had worked very hard to organize the battlefield and draw the North and South sections, with the river between, but he could not achieve his goal in the way most children of his age can. Looking at the picture, one cannot distinguish the river from the battleground. Ken tried to draw "A Tornado" and "A Tital Wave" and was unable to control his movements on paper; this picture was more scribbled than drawn. The scribbling eliminated all of the boundaries in this instance also.

Ken also drew "Super Rabbit" (figure 72). While this shows a little more control, the form is not consistent with images drawn by other children of his age. Here too, Ken was unable to stay within the boundaries he personally established; he was compelled to scribble in and around the figure. Ken has been receiving special attention in his school setting, including medication and art therapy. It is hoped that intervention and treatment eventually will help

Ken to function better than he did at the time he drew the picture.

Another 8-year-old boy, Dick, also was diagnosed as hyperactive. Because of his behavior it was assumed that he also suffered from minimal brain dysfunction; therefore he was placed in a special classroom. He was referred to a colleague of mine for movement therapy to help him control his hyperactive body movements. The movement therapist, Dianne Dulicai, began to suspect that this child was emotionally disturbed and did *not* have any minimal brain dysfunction.

For a number of years, Mrs. Dulicai and I have worked together, using both art and dance/movement therapy approaches with individuals, families, and groups, and training students in both modalities. It is not unusual for us to share our professional concerns, and Dick's progress reflects that colloboration.

To test Mrs. Dulicai's belief that Dick did not have minimal brain dysfunction, it was decided to ask him to make two drawings of a house—the first to be drawn very quickly and the second to take as much time as he wanted (top and bottom of figure 73). As you can see, the top drawing resembles some of the artwork made by Ken (figure 72) and does look loose and scribbled over. However, when Dick was allowed to draw at his own pace, there was no evidence of minimal brain dysfunction or, for that matter, any hyperactivity.

There was a warning signal in the way Dick drew the house and tree in unrealistic proportions. At 8, this is not typical. Further investigation confirmed the suspicion that Dick's emotional problems were interfering with his ability to learn.

Movement therapy sessions were focused on Dick's emotional problems. Counseling sessions with his mother also were held, and within the year he was able to return to a normal classroom setting.

Figure 73

9 AND 10 YEARS

At 9, Adam still prefers the company of boys, and his interests continue to center around school activities and sports. He and his friends will get together as frequently as they can during school and after. Adam is particularly pleased when he and some of his classmates are invited into a game of baseball with some of the older boys. Weather permitting, the boys will play games—basketball, kickball, street hockey, and football. Sometimes on a weekend or after dinner Adam's father or one of the other boys' fathers will join them. Adam does not always feel like playing in a game and some days is content just to watch.

When the weather brings the boys indoors, there is always television, science fiction games, or card games. Adam and his friends have their favorite rock stars and are very likely to have a radio or record player blaring regardless of what else they are doing. This does not always please the adults in the house, and compromises must be negotiated between Adam and his parents about when and where in the house he can listen to his music.

Other areas of compromise begin to occur around the issues of what Adam wants to wear to school (probably the same kinds of T-shirts and jackets his friends are wearing); what games and sports equipment he *must* have, and how much money he *needs* to "go places" with the boys on the weekend.

Lisa and her friends are not playing with their dolls as much as they did during the previous year, but the dolls are still very much part of the decor in their bedrooms. Gymnastic activities after school are appealing, and Lisa finds new friends as her interests grow. Like Adam, Lisa has her favorites among the rock stars.

Clothes are becoming an important item for Lisa. She and her friends will try to convince their parents that they *must* have a special sweater or a certain style shoe—they want very much to have the same kinds of things their peers have, and want to look like them. Lisa loves to go shopping with her mother or some of her friends on weekends. These young girls are also noticing jewelry and experimenting with makeup.

Sometimes it is necessary to squeeze in schoolwork between all of these peer activities, but most of the time Adam and Lisa realize that school is very important. They also know that if they do not give enough time to schoolwork, they will be in trouble with parents and teachers.

As the twins become age 10 and approach age 11, they realize that more and more is expected of them. Adam and Lisa are expected to do their homework; they are expected to take care of their personal hygiene; they are expected to understand why they cannot have everything they want. Parents and teachers are setting limits. Lisa and Adam are not always willing to comply, and this causes some friction between their parents and themselves. They are beginning to realize that, for now, they must accept these limits. Their parents also realize that the twins are not always pleased with them and accept that; their limit setting will eventually help the twins know their own limits as responsible adults.

There are other important and interesting things happening at this time. Adam and Lisa and their friends are becoming more aware of their bodies. They notice some of the girls growing taller faster than the boys, and some of the girls developing breasts. Privately, the girls discuss menstruation and its relation to having babies. When not able to find an answer to a particular question about these subjects, Lisa will ask her mother to explain. Adam will pose his questions to his father.

Some 9- to 10-year-olds attend boy-girl parties, but they are not much fun. The boys sit in one corner and clown around while the girls sit in another, giggling and trying to decide how to get the boys to dance. At this age children still are not ready to socialize with peers of the opposite sex.

This is a time of preadolescent anxiety—some of Lisa's and Adam's friends long to jump into adolescence, and others are holding back. The twins notice that some friends *act* older and leave them behind; others now seem too young for them.

Intellectually the twins are developing learning skills that enable them to follow a thought process from beginning to end. They can identify new learning problems and understand new ways to solve them. They know, for example, that pouring a glass of water into different-sized bottles does not change the *amount* of water; they can put objects in size order, for example, smallest to largest, and then reverse the process.

The art productions of 9- and 10-year-olds will show that this is a time when familiar objects are represented realistically. Baselines are elevated and ground lines are clearly drawn. Objects and people are illustrated in frontal and profile views and will show action. People and objects in the environment will be in realistic proportion to each other. The subject matter will show us the facts the children are learning and their fantasies as they move through later childhood and approach the normal upheaval of adolescence.

Some of Adam's and Lisa's real-life counterparts show us these facts and fantasies in their drawings.

Like some pictures we saw previously in this chapter, the first seven art productions described were created by children from the Dade County Public Schools in Miami, Florida, and represent different ethnic and religious backgrounds. We know nothing about these children except their age and sex—and what they tell us about themselves in their pictures.

Figure 74

Vera, 9, knew quite a bit about baseball. She drew a baseball player "up to bat" (figure 74). He is standing on the base, feet in position, arms up, and bat ready to swing. His baseball uniform is handsomely painted in red and white. Vera also knew sky meets ground, and she was able to keep the paint from smearing, so that everything she wanted to say was carefully and clearly illustrated.

Rita, 9 was interested in sports, too. She told us about two girls and a boy playing football on a field of grass. One girl appeared to be getting ready to kick, the other girl reminds us of a cheerleader, and the boy on the side is holding a football. Rita's figures are all in motion and in realistic proportion to each other. Her decision to show just *three* players leads us to believe that Rita may still have been working through her transition from home to school and peers; this is *not* unusual for this age. Rita's painting does show us that she was at the proper cognitive and social levels for her age.

Jose, 9, seemed to have a real appreciation for flowers. He creatively painted a pink flower with a yellow center, placing it on a blue background. The way Jose used all the space on the paper and applied the paint with sweeping brush strokes tells us that he has been encouraged to express himself creatively and had acquired the necessary skills to do so.

Aaron, at 9, has discovered prize fighting. His drawing of two prize fighters and the referee is remarkably detailed for a child of his age (figure 75). Aaron showed one fighter knocked to the canvas; the other fighter is being proclaimed the winner by the referee, who is also announcing this feat over a microphone. Aaron has missed no detail, and the smile on the winner's face tells us that this young artist felt good about himself. Aaron should have felt pleased—his drawing shows that he was functioning on an advanced intellectual level and could clearly represent anything he chose.

At 9, Bert was as capable as Jose in depicting people and objects in his environment that interest him. Bert's drawing showed a room equipped with a worktable, shelves, desk, and desk chair, in which a man and woman are working. The realistic way Bert drew one figure facing front and the other figure in profile, both holding objects,

Figure 75

showed that Bert's artistic skills and learning ability were better than average when this picture was produced.

Cathy, 9, painted a colorful picture of three women, all dressed brightly and in different positions. We cannot tell whether Cathy's figures are dancing or walking, and we are not quite sure what two of the women are holding. Cathy seemed to have a little more difficulty in handling paint than did some of her peers, but her organized, creative composition communicated that Cathy knew what she wanted to express and was doing it well for her age.

Sheila, 9, told a story about a girl walking along a street, pulling a small child in a wagon. We do not know whether Sheila has a young brother or sister or is romanticizing about growing up and pulling her own child in a wagon. She wrote the word "love" on the top step leading to the door of the house drawn behind the figures. Sheila's picture, so carefully executed, says to us that this scene was very important to her and that she was capable of expressing herself creatively.

The seven children whose pictures we just discussed have shown us, through their artistic productions, their own unique and individual interests. The way in which they are able to express these interests tells us that they show developmental progress normal for their age. Some are a little more advanced than others, which may mean that some children are able to learn more easily than others and have had more encouragement to be creative; some children are moving along the developmental path a little more slowly, at their own pace.

You met Elysa when she was 8½. At that time we mentioned that she had not yet learned to represent a horizon line, and at 9½ she was still separating sky and ground in her drawings. In a drawing given to us, Elysa has drawn a two-sided house. There were two paths, one leading to the front door and the other going around to the back of the house. The house is firmly set on ground that seems to be bordered by water. There are trees, an object in the water, sky above, and a sun. At this age, Elysa was continuing to develop her ability to represent her surroundings and pay more attention to details.

By age 10, Elysa had caught up with her peers and perhaps was even moving ahead of them. For a school project she created an intricate design in black and white. The elaborate and sophisticated way in which Elysa solved this assignment revealed that she was able to address problems on an advanced intellectual level. Elysa could also tell us that she was approaching adolescence with *normal* concerns about herself. In another drawing given to us, she showed a figure in profile leaning on a raised knee. The mouth was drawn so that it almost looks like a moustache; there is an earring on the ear. It is not unusual for a child of this age to begin to draw figures that combine female and male characteristics. Adolescence is a time when this question of identity must be faced once again. At 10, Elysa's figure drawing suggests that she was not yet ready to "face" this task or to "move" too quickly—one foot was eliminated by the bottom of the page.

We already presented Dayna's drawings at age 4 (figure 14) and 7 (figure 60). In these artworks she expressed her fantasies and activities, as do other children her age. At 9, however, Dayna produced a crayon drawing that is at once colorful, free, and tightly controlled—and very different from her other pictures. This picture reminded me of Scott's drawing produced when he was anxious about his father's absence (figure 69). I could not help wondering whether Dayna's image also expressed concern about a real or imagined loss. Some months later, I learned the answer from Dayna's mother. The family's beloved housekeeper, who had been with the family since Dayna was an infant, had retired around the time Dayna did this picture. Unlike Scott, Dayna felt a real loss and, like Scott, was filling in different areas and shapes with heavy crayon lines; this was a way to "contain" the feelings connected with this separation.

Children in the 9- to 10-year-old age group enjoy creating images of different real and fantasized characters— some funny and some unbelievable and even weird. This is one way they imaginatively express thoughts and feelings about who they will be (or not be) when they grow up.

Keith, 9, has been drawing fantasy characters for months. In fact, while this work was in process, he and three of his friends sent us a book of characters they created and titled "THE DUDES." You have seen Keith's artwork at age 4 (figures 42 and 43), age 5 (figure 48), and age 7 (figure 61). At 9, Keith has drawn a strange-looking character, with one green eye and one red eye, with a red high hat perched on the side of his head (figure 76). Keith called his picture "Jamaican Jugee." This "person" in Keith's picture is kneeling on a green hill, high above everything—his head and most of his body are in the clouds. The colors and the objects have been applied with great care. We do not know what this figure meant to Keith, but we learned that he spent days completing it.

Figure 76

Figure 77

Another character created by Keith, named "Jamaican Juji," was elaborately detailed in pencil. This figure has hair standing on end, bloodshot eyes, and a mouth that appears to be screaming. "Juji" seems to be shocked by what he sees, and he is not nearly so "lofty" as is Keith's "Jamaican Jugee." What fantasies of Keith's this figure reflects are also unknown to us. But both drawings tell us that this child was able to show us intellectually and emotionally his wildest fantasies in a way that is acceptable and appropriate for his age.

At 9, Milton, Keith's friend and co-creator of "THE DUDES," created "BUBBA" (figure 77). With two sets of ears, squiggly hair, wrinkled brow, and odd features, "BUBBA" does not look like anyone we know. The drawing does tell us that the artist who produced this is very clever and imaginative for his age.

The other co-creators of "THE DUDES" happened to be 11, and we include them here to demonstrate how different, and at the same time similar, children are between 9 and 11 years.

Simon, 11, chose to make a female character called "Shirley." She has pigtails, wide eyes, and a most unusual body (figure 78). Simon has learned to shade objects with a pencil, giving dimension to the face he has drawn. Although the facial features are feminine, there is little hint that the body is female. This is not surprising, for Simon was closer to adolescence than were Keith and Milton. Like Elysa, mentioned above, he was probably beginning to be aware of some of the tasks, related to his physical development, that he would have to "face."

Figure 78

Alan, also 11, avoided the issue of doing a male or female character. Instead, he drew a "Peanut Head" with droopy eyes, odd nose, and mouth with a cigar hanging out of one side (figure 79). The caricature also has a skinny neck, but no torso.

All four of these boys have cleverly allowed us a glimpse of their fanciful views of themselves and others—at least during the week they spent producing "THE DUDES."

Another boy between ages 9 and 10 had an entirely different style to communicate his thoughts and feelings consistent with this age. Don drew two pictures at the request of his teacher. The first was a spontaneous drawing of a huge figure with a pumpkin head, standing over a figure that has been stabbed. Feelings of aggression and

Figure 79

anger are normal at this age, and Don knew by now that to express them directly was not acceptable. But he also knew that by creating unreal characters he could express any of his feelings on paper.

Don's second picture was a family portrait. It is clear in this image that he did not view his sisters (females) in the same way he viewed himself, his parents, and his brothers. His sisters barely look human, while everyone else seems to have a very normal face. He omitted all human bodies, but drew a huge dog (no doubt the family pet) almost complete at the bottom of the page. We have said before that omission of body parts at specific ages is a warning signal. However, we know that Don can draw very realistically when he wants to, and at this preadolescent stage it is *not* unusual to see incomplete figures.

WARNING SIGNALS AT 9 AND 10

Anne, 10, was in Don's class and also did a family portrait for her teacher. At first glance we were impressed with Anne's ability to draw very detailed and complete figures. However, the teacher's note on the picture told us that Ann had several unrealistic excuses for not including herself—"she didn't fit," "she couldn't draw self," and did so only on the third request. We also noticed that she put herself at a distance from the rest of the family, everyone is floating in space, and there is a sun in the upper right. Children this age are confronted with the need to gain distance from their families as they come closer to adolescence, but Anne's reluctance to include herself at all, the absence of a ground line, and the presence of the sun drawn like that of a very young child, in contrast to the very sophisticated way she drew the figures, point to inconsistencies that warrant close observation of Anne's behavior and her interactions with peers and adults.

Another child in the same class as Don and Anne had drawn a picture that raised many concerns about her intellectual and emotional development. Elaine, 9, drew a tree, a rainbow, birds, and a cloud. These images are typical of those produced by children around age 4 and 5 years. This is a warning signal that something may be wrong.

Mickey and Pam, 9 years old, also showed cause for concern in the way they illustrated their families. Mickey drew stick figures without any hands or feet. We have said that omissions at this age are not unusual, but the floating forms, her childlike attempt to distinguish between females and males, and the "potato head" faces all suggest that Mickey was functioning on a level much lower than his chronological age. Pam did put a ground line under her family figures, but they were drawn like those of a child aged 5 or 6. Both of these children's pictures contain serious warning signals.

We do know something about Jason, 10. He moved from a rural community to an urban one and was sent to a special school for the learning disabled. One of his early drawings, produced for the art therapist in his school, led the staff to believe that Jason's immaturity and stress over the family's recent move caused his learning problems—not brain damage as suspected at first. In this instance the warning signals in Jason's drawings helped to define the origin of his problems. His classroom teachers and art therapist worked together to help this child "ground" himself in his new and frightening environment—the city.

A discussion of his drawings tells us how Jason progressed over the next year. In the first one we saw, he used his fingers, covered with charcoal, to make circles above the scribbled ground. His next picture had much more ground, and the sun made a partial appearance in the upper corner. Jason then began to make images that told us he could represent realistic objects in proportion to each other, with a ground line under them. The last drawing, illustrating a wonderful improvement, showed a house, a tree, a smiling little boy, and a snowman, all grounded and in proportion to each other. This picture, seen without benefit of the others and without information about this child, would surely be a warning signal. Jason was still not functioning at the level of his peers, but with support he could continue to progress and gain some of the intellectual and emotional skills needed to handle the challenges of adolescence.

Chapter 8

The End of
the Beginning

By the time children reach age 11, they are approaching the end of those developmental stages/sequences that must prepare them for the upheaval of adolescence and eventual adulthood. Childhood is behind them. Most appropriately for this kind of book, the critical first decade of a child's life can be described very well through a child's picture.

I am fairly certain that Brent, 11, was *not* thinking of either childhood or adolescence when he produced a Halloween picture for a school competition—he was thinking of winning the competition and having his drawing hung in the hallway of his school (figure 80). Brent drew a ghost orchestra. The conductor, with his back to the viewer, stands inside an open gate facing the musicians who sit on tombstones and play their instruments. Skeletons dance in the background, and tree stumps have smiling faces. Brent has woven his name above the clouds. We do not know whether the ghosts represent the past or the future, but Brent has drawn himself on a *threshold,* not looking behind and facing the unknown. On the back of the picture Brent explained that his inspiration for this was a musical composition, *La Danse Macabre* by Saint-Saëns.

Figure 80

You have met Brent many times before and know that now he has the skills to orchestrate his way through *his* gate and *his* dance.

We think of another child who was not so fortunate as Brent and many of the other normal children presented in these pages. Pat was a 17-year-old "child" when I met her in a state hospital many years ago. She had been diagnosed as schizophrenic, and the staff considered her a problem patient because she was uncooperative. She did like to draw flowers and figures and fill in squares. One of my students brought Pat's drawings to my attention because they did not seem to be typical of those produced by other schizophrenic patients. They were not; they were like those frequently produced by mentally retarded adults. An example of Pat's work was a drawing of a little girl with outstretched arms, standing in the middle of a number of blocks. Pat could not write her name correctly and could not stay within the lines of her blocks. Psychological testing confirmed that Pat was brain damaged, and her "uncooperativeness" was a manifestation of both her inability to learn and her frustration. At 17, Pat did not have the skills to "orchestrate" her future.

These examples help to remind us about the point of this book—learning, through examples provided by their creative expressions, how to lead your children in the early years, so they can learn to lead themselves.

Mastering developmental tasks in the earlier years is critical for the child entering adolescence, a naturally difficult time between the ages of 11 and 17. This phase of development would require another book. But keep in mind that it is a time for children to test new limits, find new role models to help them become independent and define their own identity, and separate from their parents. Adolescence is normally chaotic, but without the mastery of the first ten years, the adolescent cannot make order out of later chaos.

Picture an army of soldiers traveling through a war zone. They win some battles and they lose some—and some of the soldiers never get through. Now think of an infant, equipped with a normal capacity for growth. If problems encountered along the way are not resolved, the infant will not have all the skills (soldiers) needed to handle the everyday problems of living.

Another issue of concern is the sexual abuse of children. There is no place in this book to properly address this subject, but in recent years a number of articles have appeared in newspapers and professional journals, strongly suggesting that a particular image drawn by a child *tells* us that the child has been sexually abused. For example, if a child draws a large figure with enormous hands, that may be a representation of an abusive person in that child's environment. At present we do not have sufficient information to allow us to say we can "see" evidence of *specific* physical or sexual abuse in children's *free, non-directed* drawings. We can see indicators of "children at risk" in spontaneous drawings; such drawings have been shown and discussed throughout this book. When *directed* by qualified professionals, children will draw realistic and/ or symbolic representations of abuses they have endured. These expressions are especially useful in helping children to express and deal with these traumatic events.

A number of years ago, I was privileged to work with a very sensitive and creative psychiatric nurse. She became familiar with the use of art psychotherapy for severely disturbed adults, and we often discussed how, for many of these patients, it was the first time in years that they were expressing themselves creatively. The following poem, given to me as a gift from this nurse, is *her* creative expression of the sadness she felt for those who had been inhibited in their own artistic expressions.

> I could not talk
> and so I drew
> on the floor, with chalk,
> When I was small.
>
> I tried to tell you—you didn't know.
> Poor soul!
>
> I could not talk
> and so I sketched
> on paper, with charcoal,
> When I was young.
>
> I tried to show you—you didn't see.
> Poor soul!
>
> I could not talk
> and so I painted
> on canvas, with oil,
> When I was grown.
>
> I tried to reach you—you didn't understand.
> Poor soul!

I could not talk
and so I created
on clay, with my hands,
When I was old.

I tried, too late!
You can no longer feel what I say.

Jeanne Byrne Kosek

Appendix

Sources of Professional Help

Facilities

Clinics in hospitals and medical schools
Private clinics
State clinics
Clinics associated with colleges and universities that offer specialized programs in psychology, the arts in therapy, and related fields
Public schools

Professional Personnel

Pediatrician
Family physician
Clinical psychologist
School psychologist
Psychologist who specializes in testing procedures
Psychiatrist
Psychoanalyst
Art psychotherapist
Speech therapist
Dance/movement therapist
Music therapist
Occupational therapist

Organizations

American Art Therapy Association
11800 Sunrise Valley Drive, Suite 808
Reston, VA 22091

American Association of Music Therapy
66 Morris Avenue
Springfield, NJ 07081

American Dance Therapy Association
2000 Century Plaza, Suite 230
Columbia, MD 21044

American Medical Association
535 N. Dearborn Street
Chicago, IL 60610

Local medical society
Refer to local telephone directory

American Orthopsychiatry Association
19 West 44th Street, Suite 1616
New York, NY 10036

American Psychiatric Association
1700 18th Street, NW
Washington, DC 20009

American Psychological Association
122 17th Street, NW
Washington, DC 20036

American Speech-Language-Hearing Association
1080 Rockville Pike
Rockville, MD 20852

Council for Exceptional Children
1920 Association Drive
Reston, VA 22091

National Association of Music Therapy
1133 15th Street, NW
Washington, DC 20005

U.S. Department of Education
400 Maryland Avenue, SW
Washington, D.C. 20202

Local board of education
Refer to local telephone directory

U.S. Department of Health and Human Services
200 Independence Avenue, SW
Washington, DC 20201

Bibliography

Alshuler, R. H., and L. W. Hattwick. *Painting and Personality.* Chicago: University of Chicago Press, 1947 (rev. ed., 1969).

Arnheim, R. *Art and Visual Perception.* Berkeley: University of California Press, 1954 (rev. ed., 1974).

Arnheim, R. *Visual Thinking.* Berkeley: University of California Press, 1969.

Axline, V. M. *Dibs in Search of Self.* Boston: Houghton Mifflin, 1966.

Bettelheim, B. *Love Is Not Enough.* Illinois: The Free Press, 1950.

Bruner, J. S. "The Course of Cognitive Growth." *American Psychologist* 19 (1964):1–15.

Coles, R. *Erick Erikson, The Growth of His Work.* Boston: Little Brown, 1970.

Decarie, T. Goyin. *Intelligence and Affectivity in Early Childhood.* New York: International Universities Press, 1965.

DiLeo, J. H. *Young Children and Their Drawings.* New York: Bruner/Mazel, 1970.

DiLeo, J. H. *Children's Drawings as Diagnostic Aids.* New York: Bruner/Mazel, 1973.

Fink, P. J., M. J. Goldman, and M. F. Levick. "Art Therapy, A New Discipline." *Pennsylvania Medicine* 70 (1967):60–66.

Fraiberg, S. *The Magic Years.* New York: Charles Scribner Sons, 1959.

Freud, A. "Normality and Pathology in Childhood: Assessments of Development." *The Writings of Anna Freud.* Vol. 6. New York: International Universities Press, 1965.

Furth, H. G. *Thinking Without Language.* Englewood Cliffs, N.J.: Prentice-Hall, 1966.

Gantt, L., and M. Strauss. *Art Therapy—A Bibliography, January 1940–June 1973*. National Institute of Mental Health, 1974.

Gardner, H. *The Arts and Human Development*. New York: John Wiley and Sons, 1973.

Greenspan, S. I. "Intelligence and Adaptation." In *Psychological Issues*, edited by H. J. Schlesinger. New York: International Universities Press, Inc., 1979, 12, 3/4.

Haber, R. N. "Where Are the Visions in Visual Perception?" In *Imagery—Current Cognitive Approaches*, edited by S. J. Segal. New York: Academic Press, 1971, 36–48.

Hammer, E. F. *The Clinical Application of Projective Drawing*. 2d ed. Springfield, Ill: Charles C Thomas, 1978.

Hardiman, G. W., and T. Zernich. "Some Considerations of Piaget's Cognitive-Structuralist Theory and Children's Artistic Development." *Studies in Art Education* 23 (1980):3.

Horowitz, M. J. *Image Formation and Cognition*. New York: Appleton-Century-Crofts, 1970.

Inhelder, B., and J. Piaget. *The Growth of Logical Thinking From Childhood to Adolescence*. Translated by A. Parsons and S. Milgram. New York: Basic Books, 1958 (originally published, 1955).

Kellogg, R. with S. O'Dell. *The Psychology of Children's Art*. CRM—Random House Publication, 1967.

Kellogg, R. *Analyzing Children's Art*. Palo Alto, California: Mayfield Publishing Co., 1969, 1970.

Kestenberg, J. S. *Children and Parents: Psychoanalytic Studies in Development*. New York: Jason Aronson, 1975.

Koppitz, E. M. *Psychological Evaluation of Children's Human Figure Drawings*. New York: Grune & Stratton, 1968.

Kramer, E. *Art Therapy in a Children's Community*. Springfield, Ill.: Charles C Thomas, 1958.

Kwiatkowska, H. *Family Therapy and Evaluation Through Art*. Springfield, Ill.: Charles C Thomas, 1978.

Lewis, M. M. *Language, Thought, and Personality*. New York: Basic Books, 1963.

Levick, M. F. "The Goals of the Art Therapist as Compared to Those of the Art Teacher." *Journal of Albert Einstein Medical Center* 15 (1967):157–170.

Levick, M. F. "Family Art Therapy in the Community." *Philadelphia Medicine* 69 (1973):257–261.

Levick, M. F. "Art in Psychotherapy." In *Current Psychotherapies,* edited by J. Masserman. New York: Grune & Stratton, 1975.

Levick, M. F. *They Could Not Talk and So They Drew.* Springfield, Ill.: Charles C Thomas, 1983.

Levick, M. F., and J. Herring. "Family Dynamics—As Seen Through Art Therapy." *Art Psychotherapy* 1 (1973):45–54.

Levick, M. F., D. Dulicai, C. Briggs, and I. Billock. "The Creative Arts Therapies." In *A Handbook for Specific Learning Disabilities,* edited by W. Adamson and K. Adamson. New York: Gardner Press, 1979.

Lowenfeld, V. *Creative and Mental Growth.* 3rd ed. New York: Macmillan, 1957.

Machover, K. *Personality Projection in the Drawing of the Human Figure.* 2d ed. Springfield, Ill.: Charles C Thomas, 1978.

Mahler, M., F. Pine, and A. Bergman. *The Psychological Birth of the Human Infant.* New York: Basic Books, 1975.

Naumburg, M. *Studies of Free Art Expression in Behavior of Children as a Means of Diagnosis and Therapy.* New York: Coolidge Foundation, 1947.

Odier, C. *Anxiety and Magical Thinking.* New York: International Universities Press, 1956.

Piaget, I. *Play, Dreams, and Imitation in Childhood.* Translated by C. Gattegno and F. M. Hodgson. New York: W. W. Norton, 1962 (originally published, 1946).

Rubin, J. A. *Child Art Therapy.* New York: Van Nostrand, Reinhold, 1978.

Winnicott, D. W. *Playing and Reality.* New York: Basic Books, 1971.

About the Author

Myra F. Levick postponed pursuing her own art career education to work while her husband was in medical school. In 1958, when their third and youngest daughter was in second grade, her husband encouraged Dr. Levick to resume her studies, and she obtained a Bachelor of Fine Arts degree (B.F.A.) from Moore College of Art in Philadelphia.

Unwilling to commit herself to the very isolated existence of being a painter, Dr. Levick planned to continue graduate study for a master's degree in the history of art. However, she became intrigued by the idea, proposed by the late Morris J. Goldman, M.D., of working in the psychiatric unit at the Albert Einstein Medical Center, Northern Division, a general hospital in Philadelphia. Dr. Goldman was the director of this unit, the first unlocked ward in a general hospital, and was convinced of the value of having an artist work with mentally ill patients. While Dr. Levick employed her art skills in working with the patients, she also studied psychiatry and psychology, obtaining a master's degree in educational psychology (M.Ed.) from Temple University in Philadelphia.

During this time Dr. Levick and Dr. Goldman, along with Paul J. Fink, M.D., a psychoanalyst on the Einstein staff, published journal articles about their experiences in art therapy, stimulating the interests of art students, art teachers, and practicing artists to pursue training in this growing field. By 1967 Dr. Fink, who had become director of education in the department of psychiatry at Hahnemann Medical College and Hospital (now Hahnemann University) in Philadelphia, and Dr. Goldman, who had become director of the Hahnemann Mental Health Community Center, saw the need for a graduate training program in art therapy. Later that year Hahnemann initiated the first program anywhere to offer graduate-level training leading to a master's degree in art therapy.

Dr. Levick joined this group at Hahnemann to develop a course outline and to coordinate the program with art therapy activities on the psychiatric units at Hahnemann Hospital. With the support of specialists in child psychology, psychiatrists, and educators in the community, the program was offered to a continually growing student body in a variety of settings. Attracting the interest of practicing art therapists all over the country, a guest lecture series and meeting for these practitioners was sponsored by Hahnemann in 1968. This led to the establishment of the American Art Therapy Association (AATA), which approves training programs and registers art therapists. Dr. Levick ws elected its first president.

Feeling a continuing need to broaden her knowledge of her own and related fields, Dr. Levick studied family and group psychotherapy in the early 1970s and became licensed to practice art psychotherapy in Pennsylvania. She continued to study psychology, maintaining a private clinical practice along with her academic position at Hahnemann, which included teaching and supervising creative arts students, family therapy students, psychology students, and medical psychiatric residents.

In 1976 Dr. Levick was asked to design and coordinate a program at Hahnemann to provide training for art, dance/ movement, and music therapists. Initially supported by a three-year grant from the National Institute of Mental

Health, this became the model program for training creative arts therapists together in a graduate program within a medical school. Dr. Levick was named director of the program, called the Master's Creative Arts in Therapy Program (MCAT), and became a professor in the Department of Mental Health Sciences and in the medical college.

At the same time Dr. Levick continued her own academic pursuits, receiving a Ph.D. in child development from Bryn Mawr College in 1981. In 1984, seeking more time to work on this book, she relinquished her title as director of MCAT at Hahnemann, remaining in her current capacity as professor and consultant to the program.

Dr. Levick's textbook, *They Could Not Talk and So They Drew, Children's Styles of Coping and Thinking,* was published in 1983, and the investigative work for that textbook became the basis for *Mommy, Daddy, Look What I'm Saying.* Dr. Levick, widely known and respected in the fields of art therapy and psychology, has authored numerous scholarly articles and book chapters. She served as president of AATA from 1969 to 1971, has long been a member of the executive board of the association, and was named an honorary life member in 1973. She is editor-in-chief of an international professional journal, *The Arts in Psychotherapy,* and is a sought-after guest lecturer and teacher all over the world. Her major interest has always been, and remains, the education and training of students in the mental health field. But her belief in encouraging the creativity of children does not end with the classroom. As Dr. Levick herself puts it: "I believe strongly that it is not enough for art therapists to share what we have learned with our peers and students. We also need to communicate this information to those influential people—mothers, fathers, and teachers—who are responsible for shaping and molding the children of the world."

Index

189